Freelance Christianity

Freelance Christianity

Philosophy, Faith, and the Real World

VANCE G. MORGAN

CASCADE *Books* • Eugene, Oregon

FREELANCE CHRISTIANITY
Philosophy, Faith, and the Real World

Copyright © 2017 Vance G. Morgan. All rights reserved. Except for brief quotations in critical publications or reviews, no part of this book may be reproduced in any manner without prior written permission from the publisher. Write: Permissions, Wipf and Stock Publishers, 199 W. 8th Ave., Suite 3, Eugene, OR 97401.

Cascade Books
An Imprint of Wipf and Stock Publishers
199 W. 8th Ave., Suite 3
Eugene, OR 97401

www.wipfandstock.com

PAPERBACK ISBN: 978-1-4982-9913-8
HARDCOVER ISBN: 978-1-4982-9915-2
EBOOK ISBN: 978-1-4982-9914-5

Cataloguing-in-Publication data:

Names: Morgan, Vance G.

Title: Freelance Christianity : philosophy, faith, and the real world. / Vance G. Morgan.

Description: Eugene, OR: Cascade Books, 2017 | Includes bibliographical references and index.

Identifiers: ISBN 978-1-4982-9913-8 (paperback) | ISBN 978-1-4982-9915-2 (hardcover) | ISBN 978-1-4982-9914-5 (ebook)

Subjects: LCSH: 1. Philosophy and religion. | 2. Philosophy, Modern. I. Title.

Classification: BD573 .M500 2017 (print) | BD573 (ebook)

Manufactured in the U.S.A.   MAY 23, 2017

For Jeanne:
You are the sun, the moon, the stars,
and my home

Where there is love there is courage,
where there is courage there is peace,
where there is peace there is God.
And when you have God, you have everything.

—Louise Penny, *A Fatal Grace*

Table of Contents

Acknowledgements ix

Introduction—My Deepest Me 1

Chapter 1: Atheism—My Invisible Friend 7

Chapter 2: Idolatry—The Designer God Project 18

Chapter 3: Change—Living with Provisional Faith 28

Chapter 4: Attentiveness—There It Is 39

Chapter 5: Silence—Taking My Soul Wherever I Go 50

Chapter 6: Grace—Having the Right *Niyyah* 60

Chapter 7: Faith—Dealing with the "F" Word 71

Chapter 8: Prayer—What Are You Going to Do About It? 82

Chapter 9: Courage—"I'll Remember You" 92

Chapter 10: Humility—From Infinity to Intimacy 103

Chapter 11: Beauty—Where the Divine and the Human Meet 114

Chapter 12: Hope—I Will Bring You Home 124

Chapter 13: Incarnation—A Preposterous Love 135

Conclusion—Learning How to Read 145

Bibliography 153

Name Index 157

Scripture Index 160

Acknowledgements

There are dozens of people without whom this book would have never seen the light of day. The seeds of this book were sown, watered, and cultivated during a sabbatical semester that I spent during the first several months of 2009 as a resident scholar at the Collegeville Institute for Ecumenical and Cultural Research on the campus of St. John's University in Collegeville, Minnesota. Thanks to Don Ottenhof, the institute's executive director, who was a much-needed source of support and critique as I tested the waters of a new way of writing. Don was also the first who advised me to start a blog. Carla Durand and Elisa Schneider—you run a great shop!

While at Collegeville my soul came alive. It was through experiencing daily communal prayer and silence with the monks of St. John's Abbey in Collegeville that I slowly discovered a long-sought place of peace and centeredness, the "deepest me" that St. Catherine of Genoa calls "God." My sincere thanks to Abbot John Klassen, Kilian, Wilfred, Brother John, and all the monks who welcomed a spiritually tired non-Catholic with open arms into their midst several times per day. The Benedictine motto is "*Ora et Labora*"—you taught me the meaning of *Ora*.

At Collegeville I met Ivan and Lois Kauffman, a couple who became important to me, then to Jeanne, in more ways than I can count. Ivan was a fellow resident scholar—I have never known anyone with a more principled dedication to the truth and to a vibrant faith. He passed away in 2015; I learned at his funeral that we shared the same favorite verse from Scripture, the prophet Micah's directive to "do justice, love mercy, and walk humbly with your God." Ivan lived that directive to its fullest. Lois was my regular buddy at abbey prayers—out of the dozen or so people at the institute that winter and spring, Lois and I were unanimously described as the two people least likely to get sucked into the orbit of abbey prayers. But we

Acknowledgements

did. Lois and I will forever share the memories of our fifteen-minute walks in silence and minus–twenty-degree temperatures to morning prayer.

Kathleen Norris's book *The Cloister Walk* changed my life even before we met several years ago. I am grateful for her wise advice and strong support; I'm also pleased that I get to call a famous author my friend. Kathleen is a model for those who seek for God wherever she might be lurking.

Many thanks to the Living Stones seminar group, a bunch of mature and experienced New England Episcopalians at Trinity Episcopal in Pawtuxet, Rhode Island. Defying all stereotypes and odds, "the Stoners" have over the past five years become the most welcoming, honest, and loving discussion group I have ever encountered. I joke that I could read to them from the phone book and they would turn it into a fruitful discussion, and it's not an exaggeration. I've seen them turn a sow's ear into a silk purse many times. I love you guys!

Marsue Harris has been a wise advisor and valued friend ever since I told her, when I discovered at our first meeting several years ago that she is an Episcopal priest, that I had done my allotted time in church and did not intend to do any more. Boy, was I wrong. Marsue has pushed me to consider new possibilities, cautioned me when I was stretched too thin, read and commented on everything I wrote, and provided a patient ear when I needed to vent. You and Robin are the best.

None of this book—absolutely none of it—would have seen the light of day without Jeanne DiPretoro, the beautiful person with whom I have had the joy of spending the past many years. She has been my first reader, most insightful critic, and a tireless cheerleader for this book from its earliest versions to the finished product. In Plato's *Symposium*, Aristophanes says that our earliest human ancestors were split in half and scattered to the four winds by Zeus in a fit of annoyance; each of us has been driven ever since to find our lost half. I bless the evening when we found each other in my parents' living room thirty years ago.

Introduction

My Deepest Me

More than twenty years ago my wife and I went to visit some old friends, a couple who had been very important in my life before Jeanne and I met. They had been a reliable source of stability and support during one of the most difficult and challenging times of my life. In the seven or eight years since I had last seen this couple a number of big things had happened in my life, including a divorce, a bitter custody battle, a remarriage, and the completion of my PhD in Philosophy. The weekend visit was lovely, with good food and conversation, a boat trip on an Alabama lake, and church on Sunday. I had been in pretty bad shape the last time my friends had seen me, so they were thrilled to meet my beautiful new wife, to hear about my sons, and to see that I apparently was doing well.

In the middle of one conversation that weekend, one of my friends asked a question that has haunted me ever since: *how can you be a Christian and a philosopher?* Her question was sincere, without a hint of challenge or judgment. She simply wanted to know. My friend admittedly knew little about philosophy, but she'd at least heard that philosophy is the art of questioning, of asking better and better questions about the biggest possible issues. The problem, as she saw it, was that for a Christian, most if not all of these questions are already answered. Why, if as a Christian I know all of the answers to these questions, would I spend my professional life continuing to ask them and inspiring others to do the same? Why not just introduce everyone to the truth? I truly do not remember how I responded, but I'm sure it was something quick and dismissive. Her question returned me to my youth, to bumper stickers on cars in the church parking lot that read "God said it, I believe it, that settles it," to sensing from those around me that I thought too much, that I asked too many questions, that I was too smart for my own good and too big for my britches. What I needed to do was simply believe and shut up. It would make my life, and the lives of those around me, a lot easier.

As I've processed my friend's question over time, I've come to realize that the joy and fulfillment I find in the life of the mind, of academia, and of open-ended questioning is partially, at least a teeny bit, the working out of a rebellious "up yours" to everyone who sought to fit me for their straitjacket. Philosophy on the one hand, as a life-defining activity, is who I am, and I even get paid for doing it. Conservative Christianity, on the other hand, is something I was saddled with. I didn't choose it. It was part of the atmosphere I breathed from birth. My family and community were Christian, the first words I learned were Christian, the first songs I sang were Christian. One doesn't just walk away from that or shed it as a snake sheds its skin. I've never really believed someone who smugly with an air of superiority says something like "I was raised in (fill in the blank religion), but now I know better and I'm an atheist." If you were *really* raised in a religious tradition that seeped into your bones and psyche before you even became fully conscious and self-aware, then that influence does not end by simply flipping an intellectual switch.

During the first five months of 2009, I spent a sabbatical semester as a resident scholar at an ecumenical institute on the campus of St. John's University, run by the Benedictine order, in Collegeville, Minnesota. My academic plans were set; a well-defined book project was ready to be written. But upon arrival, it gradually became clear to me that something else was going on. For most of my fifty-plus years, I had struggled with the conservative, fundamentalist Protestant Christianity in which I was raised. What became clear in Minnesota was that what I thought was a long-term, low-grade spiritual dissatisfaction had become, without my being aware of it, a full-blown spiritual crisis. Beneath my introverted, overly cerebral surface my soul was asking John the Baptist's question of Jesus that he sent from Herod's dungeon—"Are you the one, or is it time to look for another?"

There are times when I just cannot believe what I get myself into. For instance, three summers ago I joined a reading group and committed to reading *War and Peace* over the three summer months at a pace of 150 pages or so per week. As if I didn't have enough to read with teaching two brand new courses during the next academic year, as well as the 24-7 demands of

Introduction

running a big academic program that never stopped, blah, blah, blah. In truth, I had a lot of fun returning to this 1,350-page novel that I had not read since my undergraduate days. When I read a great work of literature, and they don't come any greater than *War and Peace*, I always find myself resonating with a particular character, more or the less the character I would be if I were to jump into the novel. That character in *War and Peace* is Prince Andrei Nikolaevich Bolkonsky. I find Natasha, the main female character, annoying, and Pierre, the main male character, to need a good kick in the ass. But I get Andrei.

As a young twenty-something Andrei joined the Russian army as an officer and fought against the forces of Napoleon at Austerlitz. Wounded in battle and presumed dead, Andrei finds his way home to his family; shortly after, his wife dies after giving birth to their first child. Two years later and about 500 pages into the novel, Andrei is depressed, cynical, and incapable of finding joy or meaning in anything. Traveling in early spring to one of his estates, Pyotr, his footman, comments on the beauty of the April morning, the flowers, and the new leaves on the birch trees. Andrei's attention is drawn instead to a stand of stagnant fir trees, then to an apparently dead oak tree.

> With its huge ungainly limbs sprawling unsymmetrically, and its gnarled hands and fingers, it stood an aged, stern, and scornful monster among the smiling birch-trees. "Spring, love, happiness!" this oak seems to say. "Are you not weary of that stupid, meaningless, constantly repeated fraud? Always the same, and always a fraud! There is no spring, no sun, no happiness! Look at those cramped dead firs, ever the same, and at me too, sticking out my broken and barked fingers just where they have grown, whether from my back or my sides: as they have grown so I stand, and I do not believe in your hopes and your lies."[1]

And Andrei's mood and recent experiences are confirmed. "Let others—the young—yield afresh to that fraud, but we know life, our life is finished!"[2]

Andrei's oak reminds me of another oak, the massive one a hundred feet or so outside the front door of my Collegeville Institute apartment where I spent four sabbatical months a few years ago. I arrived in the middle of a Minnesota winter; although I am not prone to depression as Andrei was, I realize in retrospect that I carried deep within me a spiritual malaise

---

1. Tolstoy, *War and Peace*, 449.
2. Ibid.

and ennui that had been festering for years. My Collegeville oak looked as I felt inwardly that January—bare, cold, snow-covered, with few signs of life. Over the succeeding weeks, this oak became an inescapable presence in my life (it was the first thing I saw as I stepped out of my front door) and a metaphor for what was happening to me.

As the snow finally began to melt and spring inched closer, I found an accompanying inner thaw occurring, facilitated by the warmth of daily forays into the Liturgy of the Hours with the monks at St. John's Abbey a half mile or so up the road. As I tested the waters of daily prayer, I noticed a space of silence and peace slowly opening inside of me that I had never known. No voices, no visions, no miracles—but I was writing differently. The low-grade anger that had accompanied me for most of my life began to dissipate. I felt more and more like a whole person instead of a cardboard cutout. One March morning as I stumbled back from the common area at the institute with my morning Keurig coffee in tow, I walked up on a dozen or so deer hanging out under the oak. They had apparently been there ten minutes earlier as I emerged from my apartment half asleep and oblivious to the world on my way to the common area. As they noticed me noticing them, they gave me their unique white-assed salute as they sauntered away. Signs of spring under the oak, which was still naked.

Eventually a few of my colleagues said "you're not the same person you were when you first got here." And they were right—I wasn't. I began spending more time with the monks at prayer, often three times daily. Essays began to flow from a place I didn't recognize, but really liked. Little had changed outwardly, but everything was changing. As April came and other trees budded into their springtime growth, my oak remained apparently lifeless. Then one morning as I walked past it taking my usual shortcut to the road up to the abbey for seven o'clock morning prayer, I noticed that on the ends of its lowest and smallest twigs the first signs of new growth were emerging. "So you're alive after all, huh?" I muttered as I continued on, the same observation I had been making more and more frequently about myself as deeper and deeper spaces cracked open after a lifetime of neglect. I regularly took pictures from my front doorstep to track the oak's emergence into life and wrote essays to track my parallel inner emergence.

The oak grew into full-blown spring splendor as my sabbatical continued and it more and more became my daily touchstone. "Hey there," I would say as I walked past three or four times a day coming or going, and I imagined that if I were able to live in tree time rather than human

Introduction

time, I would have heard a deep, rumbling, ponderous, Tolkien Ent-like "Hey yourself" in return. The oak's stability and lack of hurry became my own goal as I practiced slowing down and plugging into the rhythms of the newly discovered energies within me. As the day of returning home drew near, I was worried. Would these changes be transferable to my real life? Would this space of centeredness and peace be available in the middle of a typical eighty- to ninety-hour work week in the middle of a semester? Or would these changes soon be a fond memory, to be filed in an already overfull internal regret file?

Two days before my leaving, one of the Benedictines preached at daily Mass (which I did not normally attend). In the middle of an otherwise forgettable homily, he quoted the obscure St. Catherine of Genoa, who said *"My deepest me is God."* The space of quietness, silence, and peace inside of me, the one I'd never known—is God. I was stunned. Tears filled my eyes. I tingled all over. Because what I had been looking for is here. And it *is* transferable. Trust me.

I have always known that a college professor's teaching and research should feed each other and have tried to live that out, with occasional success. That teaching and research can be mutually supporting is a challenging enough idea. But supposing that the life of the mind, especially philosophy, and faith have much to say to each other is for many, from both the intellect and faith side of the claim, beyond the pale, simply because the intellect and faith are stereotypically considered to be incompatible. At best they can be separate rooms in a home, rooms between which no one ever passes. Imagine my surprise when I discovered over several weeks of daily prayer and reading of the Psalms with a couple of dozen monks that the wall between my faith and philosophy room is an illusion—that both my mind and my faith want to inhabit the very same space. Not to argue or play a game of "who's on top," but rather to get to know each other and become equally committed to helping the guy whose house they are part of learn to live a coherent and integrated life. I have been regularly surprised over the past few years at what percolates to the surface from this collaboration of faith and intellect.

When I think of Collegeville the first image that invariably comes to mind is my oak. Growth, stability, silence, fortitude, rootedness—that oak represents all of the things that I hope to have carried at least a bit from my months in Minnesota. On the half-dozen or so return visits I have made, a visit to the oak and taking more pictures has always been a "must-do." I have never been at Collegeville during the autumn, so I do not know what Minnesota foliage is like or what colors the oak wears in late September and early October. I was raised in northern Vermont, the fall foliage capital of the universe, and in my imagination I see the oak garbed in brilliant orange, my favorite fall foliage color. Yellow or red would be okay, but I'll bet it's orange.

After Andrei encounters his oak tree in *War and Peace*, he spends several days inspecting his large land holdings, and then heads back toward his home outside of Moscow. Looking for the oak where he remembered first seeing it, he is at first confused.

> Without recognizing it he looked with admiration at the very oak he sought. The old oak, quite transfigured, spreading out a canopy of sappy dark-green foliage, stood rapt and slightly trembling in the rays of the evening sun. Neither gnarled fingers nor old scars nor old doubts and sorrows were in evidence now. Through the hard century-old bark, even where there were no twigs, leaves had sprouted such as one could hardly believe the old veteran could have produced. "Yes, it is the same oak," thought Prince Andrei, and all at once he was seized by an unreasoning spring-time feeling of joy and renewal.[3]

Over the next 850 pages, Andrei will grapple more than once with depression and sorrow. But an encounter with what Isaiah would have called an "oak of righteousness" has changed him for good. I know exactly how you feel, Andrei.

> They will be called oaks of righteousness, a planting of the LORD for the display of his splendor.[4]

---

3. Ibid., 452.
4. Isa 61:3.

1

Atheism—My Invisible Friend

Simone Weil writes that "Atheism is a purification."[1] Not where I come from. No word or phrase was more mysterious or terror-producing for a young Baptist boy than *atheist*. I certainly didn't know any, nor did my parents, nor did anyone in my extended family, nor did anyone who attended our church. But none of us knew any serial killers, either. Apparently atheists were out there somewhere, running Hollywood, teaching in secular universities, and generally sticking their thumbs in the eye of what they denied the existence of. It wasn't clear to me how an atheist could even stay alive. If God snuffed out Uzzah just for putting his hand on the ark in the Jewish Scriptures,[2] how did people who had the nerve to say "God doesn't exist" manage to last? I came to suspect that atheists were mythical creatures like unicorns and Bigfoot, until one day I heard my aunt Gloria, who had a very loud voice, whispering to my mother sotto voce in the next room about the new high school science teacher. "He spends a lot of time teaching evolution; I'll bet he's a practicing atheist."

That's a very interesting concept—a "practicing atheist." What exactly does that mean? Is that someone who is very serious about atheism, who has gone beyond the lazy "God doesn't exist" verbal stage and is actually putting this stuff into action? Does one practice atheism as I practiced the piano as a child, in hopes of becoming a concert atheist? Is the "practicing

1. Weil, *Gravity*, 104.
2. 2 Sam 6:6–8.

atheist" an atheist in training, sort of a Double-A or Triple-A newbie practicing and honing his atheist skills until he gets to the atheist big show? Does the "practicing atheist" try it out for a while to see how she likes it? I mean, I could be a "practicing" any number of things, like a practicing vegetarian. I could do it for a while, and even realize that it was good for me, but before long I'd just have to eat some meat. Given my general obsession with the "God question," maybe practicing atheism for a while would be good for the health of my soul, just as vegetarianism would be good for my bodily well-being.

Practicing atheism would put an end to creating God in my own image. There have been many gods in my lifetime, and every one of them is either a projection of myself or of the person(s) who introduced me to them.

- A now silent God who stopped communicating directly with human beings several centuries ago, once the dictation of the divine word in print was finished.
- A God who invites into the inner sanctum only those who have a special "prayer language."
- A God who does not "want any to perish, but all to come to repentance,"[3] but who at the same time is so judgmental and exclusive that the vast majority of the billions of human beings who have ever lived will end up in hell.
- An exclusively masculine God.
- A God who is more concerned with the length of male hair and female skirts than with the breadth and depth of one's spiritual hunger and desire.
- A God whose paramount concerns are one's positions on sexual orientation, abortion, or universal health care.
- A God who micromanages every detail of reality at every moment, including tsunamis, birth defects, and oil spills.
- A God who is more honored by self-reliance than by compassion for those in need.

And many more. As a practicing atheist I might still have anthropomorphic issues, but an anthropomorphic God would not be one of them.

3. 2 Pet 3:9.

Atheism—My Invisible Friend

Practicing atheism would be an effective antidote to any remaining obsession from my youth with what happens after death. We used to sing "This world is not my home, I'm just a-passin' through; if heaven's not my home, then Lord what will I do?" I don't know any atheist songs, so perhaps I should write one that draws my attention to *now*. As a child I thought that the only reason to become a Christian was to get an ironclad fire insurance policy from hell. Maybe I should love this world that *is* my home, one that I only get to live in for a short while. This is the world I've been given.

Atheism would provide me with new tools to apply to the problem of suffering and evil. Once I stop wondering why God allows the innocent to suffer, the guilty not to suffer, earthquakes to obliterate thousands, and the world generally to operate contrary to my wishes, the landscape looks quite different. Suffering exists—so does evil. The practicing atheist cannot ask "Why doesn't God do something about this?" and asks instead "What does this require of me?" A fresh look at my world without God-tinted lenses reveals that suffering and violence are inextricably tangled with beauty. A practicing atheist recommends a certain Stoic embrace of reality, rather than a childish affirmation of the parts I like and an impotent resistance to those I don't.

Atheism would make it much more difficult for me to seek false consolation for disappointments, difficulties, and perceived injustices. I am reminded, year after year, that a significant majority of my students, many of whom are parochial school educated, believe that consolation is the only real reason to believe in God. But consolation, although emotionally attractive, is almost always an attractive lie. If my only response to human pain, mine or someone else's, is that "the sufferings of this present time are not worth comparing with the glory about to be revealed in us,"[4] then pretty soon I become incapable of even seeing much of the suffering around me. There are times when Albert Camus's project in *The Myth of Sisyphus*, "to see if I can live without appeal,"[5] has to be *my* project. What if this is all there is? What if the only responses available to suffering and pain are *ours*? What if I don't get to pass the buck on to the divine?

"Atheism is a purification" is not a call to become an atheist. Rather, for me a serious season of practicing atheism would serve as a purgative, a process of spiritual cleansing, eliminating loose vocabulary, sloppy habits, and lazy certainties that dull my spiritual sensibilities. If my Christian faith

---

4. Rom 8:18.
5. Camus, *Sisyphus*, 53.

means anything, it means God in the flesh, incarnated in all features of this difficult, troublesome, exhilarating, and precious world that is a divine gift. Christianity will not be fully incarnated until it is joined with a respect and reverence for this world. Practicing atheism might help.

One morning, in response to a recent blog post, a friend and colleague sent me the following email:

> One thing I've been struggling with . . . is the (im)possibility of certainty in the realm of religious belief/faith. How does one lead a religious/faithful life without "certainty" that God exists, for example? Does one's faith in God amount to a kind of certainty? If it doesn't, how can it stand on a firm foundation?

Great questions—how *does* one verify that one's supposed relationship with the divine is something other than a case of one hand clapping? A popular meme among atheists is to describe the differences between various religions as a debate about whose invisible friend is more powerful. Many children have invisible friends (I did), yet this is something one supposedly grows out of or gets over. Yet there are billions of human beings who shape their whole reality and might even stake their lives on the premise that a certain invisible friend not only exists but plays an exceptionally important role in our understanding of ourselves and the reality we find ourselves in. I am one of those billions of human beings. So have I simply transferred my childhood attachment to my invisible friend to a far more interesting and complex imaginary friend who is no more real than my childhood pal? Didn't a text supposedly inspired by this cosmic imaginary friend suggest that when one becomes an adult, one is supposed to put away childish things?

Exactly how do we gather evidence for the existence of something? When is it appropriate to believe in something whose existence you have not verified in the usual, direct sensory ways? This issue often arises in philosophy classrooms. When it does, I ask my students, "How many of you believe in the existence of Mongolia?" All hands go up. "How many of you have ever been to Mongolia?" No hands go up. Then "How do you know that Mongolia exists?" My students generally provide a number of sensible reasons:

- Because I have read about Mongolia in a book or online in stories written by people who have been there (although the authors of these sources might be lying).
- Because I have seen pictures of Mongolia (even though we know that pictures can easily be misidentified or photoshopped).
- Because someone I know has been to Mongolia and told me about it (although this trusted source might be bullshitting me just for the fun of it).

The purpose of the exercise is to demonstrate that we believe in the existence of thousands of things that we have not experienced directly. The testimony of others, although not perfect or entirely reliable, serves as a reasonably solid foundation for much of what we believe. Life is too short and human capabilities are too limited to include in our collection of existential belief commitments only those items that we have experienced directly ourselves.

For many, belief in the existence of what is greater than us—what some dismiss as an "imaginary friend"—begins in exactly the same way. The sacred texts of the great monotheistic religions are accounts of what people over the centuries have believed concerning the divine. This does not prove that something greater than us exists, any more than Wikipedia entries about Mongolia prove the existence of Mongolia, but they are a good place to start. There is no reason to dismiss them just because they are referring to something that I lack direct experience of. For instance, I believed in the existence of Notre Dame Cathedral in Paris for decades before I actually saw and walked around inside it for the first time. But I suspect I would have continued to believe in the cathedral's existence even if I had never seen it myself. The indirect and secondhand evidence for its existence is just too overwhelming. So it goes with God—it's difficult to dismiss theism as a pervasive "imaginary friend" phenomenon when the reports are so consistent and pervasive.

But there's nothing better than direct encounter. In my favorite book from the Jewish Scriptures, Job expresses it well. After decades of believing in God because of secondary evidence passed down over the generations, in the midst of intense pain and suffering he encounters the real deal. "I had heard of you by the hearing of the ear," Job says, "but now my eye sees you."[6] First-person contact trumps any number of secondary sources, but does not negate those sources—it gives them new meaning and energy. How do

6. Job 42:5.

I know that God is not a figment of my imagination? The best evidence of divine reality is a changed life. I can organize the story of my life around the "before and after" of that encounter spread over several months a number of years ago. I'm not interested in proselytizing or evangelization—you should believe what your own experience can support. But as the formerly afflicted man in the Gospels says, "I was blind, but now I see." That's my story, and I'm sticking to it.

The New York Times recently published a series of interviews on its "Opinionator" blog in which Gary Gutting, a professor of philosophy at the University of Notre Dame, explores the topic of whether belief in something greater than ourselves is rational with several contemporary academics whose work intersects with such questions. One of these interviews was with Louise Antony, a professor of philosophy at the University of Massachusetts at Amherst; she represented the hardcore atheist position among Gutting's six interviewees. In response to Gutting's query as to why she is an atheist, going beyond the agnostic position that we cannot know whether God exists or not to the more definitive position that one can know that God does not exist, Antony explains:

> When I claim to know that there is no God, I mean that the question is settled to my satisfaction. I don't have any doubts. . . . The main issue is supernaturalism—I deny that there are beings or phenomena outside the scope of natural law.[7]

I must confess that I found much of the succeeding conversation to be tiresome and spinning its wheels in bottomless intellectual ruts. Antony only accepts a specific type of evidence—that which can be verified within the parameters of the laws of nature. "Aha!" I thought. She's trying to play the "seeking after God" game using a set of rules that guarantees that she will lose the game. That's like playing Monopoly using rules that guarantee you'll not proceed past Vermont Avenue. Never a good idea.

The theist makes a serious mistake when she or he agrees to play the "does God exist?" game by rules that are within "the scope of natural law," by which Antony means "laws that hard science will accept." In truth, Antony's belief that "everything is the product of mindless natural laws acting on mindless matter"[8] operating according to the inexorable laws of

---

7. Gutting and Antony, "Arguments Against God," lines 18–20.
8. Ibid., lines 103–4.

nature is as much an act of faith as the theist's belief that there is at least one being—God—that transcends those laws. In truth, I find this belief from someone who shares my profession to be sad, simply because the continuing, but usually unspoken, assumption is not only that everything, and I mean *everything*, is subject to logical scrutiny (that's fine), but also that only those things that are at least in theory within the range and scope of human reason are worthy of even a moment of human attention. It is as if humans have no other tools available for engaging with and trying to shape a meaningful life within the world where we find ourselves so unexpectedly placed.

Of greater interest is Antony's claim that "the question is settled to my satisfaction," because this raises the threshold of conviction question. Just how convinced does someone have to be of the truth of something before further investigation is stopped? Is the threshold of conviction different from person to person? And if so, how can a person with a low threshold of conviction fruitfully converse with the doubter or skeptic whose threshold is significantly higher? Gutting and Antony's conversation shifts in this direction when it moves its focus from scientific to experiential evidence. Gutting asks "What do you make of the claim from many theists that the best evidence for the existence of something greater than us is direct religious experience?"[9] After first denying that she has had such experiences, Antony offers a connective bridge that many atheists refuse to consider.

> O.K., if you hold my feet to the fire, I'll admit that I believe I know what sort of experiences the theists are talking about, that I've had such experiences, but I don't think they have the content the theists assign to them. I've certainly had experiences I would call "profound." . . . I've been tremendously moved by demonstrations of personal courage (not mine!), generosity, sympathy. I've had profound experiences of solidarity, when I feel I'm really together with other people working for some common goal. These are very exhilarating and inspiring experiences, but they are very clearly about human beings—human beings at their best.[10]

Shifting the conversation from the ways in which we describe our experiences to the content of those experiences offers an opportunity for new understanding. As a theist, I entirely share Antony's inspiration and exhilaration when experiencing human beings at their best, since this is precisely

9. Ibid., lines 115–17.
10. Ibid., lines 123–33.

where, if anywhere, one is likely to find evidence of the divine—incarnated in human activity.

Antony's comments remind me of a long-standing problem that I had with my Baptist minister father well into my adulthood. From my earliest memories, he peppered his conversations with phrases like "God told me that . . .," "the Lord directed me to . . .," and "I was going to . . . , but God told me not to," giving the impression that he and the divine had a direct line of communication others did not have access to. Knowing that I had no such direct line, I had no idea what the experience of talking directly to God was like. After many years of first thinking I was my father's spiritual inferior, then thinking that he was simply nuts, one day in my early thirties, in response to yet another "God told me that" pronouncement, I confronted him. "You say that all the time—what exactly does it feel or sound like when God says something to you?" Taken aback by what he perceived as an attack from his passive, introverted son, he grew defensive. "Well, you know, it's a strong feeling, an intuition, a sense that I should do this rather than that." "It's not a voice?" I asked. "No—it hasn't been yet, at least," he replied. "I know what those sorts of experiences are like," I sputtered—"I just don't call them God talking to me!" And for the first time we had come to at least a partial truce. Our failure to communicate was the result of vastly different language, not vastly different experiences.

Not long ago I made the rare choice to get involved in a Facebook discussion. In the midst of it, a Facebook acquaintance (whom I've never met) said "Faith is belief without evidence. What else does it mean? Why else would it be needed?" My quick and inadequate response was "Faith is not belief without evidence. Faith is belief when evidence may point in a particular direction but is not complete or exhaustive. Belief entirely without any evidence at all is simply foolishness. That foolishness is not confined to religious activities—it is rampant in politics or any other arena of belief. Non-theists are just as capable of such foolishness as theists are." As long as faith opponents are rejecting a definition of faith similar to Mark Twain's "Faith is believing something you know ain't true," I'm with them. But that's not what real faith is. Rather, it is applying the very common human activity of believing on the basis of important but partial evidence to the realm of the relationship between human and divine. The relationship between faith, evidence, knowledge, and hope is one worthy of extended investigation. But to assume at the outset that faith and evidence have nothing to do with each other is to define the game out of existence—or to guarantee advancing no further than Vermont Avenue.

During Holy Week a few years ago at our Episcopal church, the rector decided for the first time in her many years as a priest to do the Holy Saturday liturgy. It's a tough sell to get people to church on any Saturday except for a wedding or funeral, particularly during Holy Week when the most dedicated may have already been in church two or three times in the previous few days. I was one of only a few people present; if any of us had possessed the presence of mind to check the prayer book before coming, we probably wouldn't have bothered. It's a very dark liturgy. Jesus is dead in the tomb, the altar is stripped bare, and everything in the rubric is intended to get you *not* to think about what is coming the next day. A central line in one of the prayers that day was "In the midst of life we are in death." Most striking that afternoon, however, was the following from the book of Job:

> A mortal, born of woman, few of days and full of trouble comes up like a flower and withers, flees like a shadow and does not last . . . . For there is hope for a tree, if it is cut down, that it will sprout again, and that its shoots will not cease . . . . But mortals die, and are laid low; humans expire, and where are they? As waters fail from a lake, and a river wastes away and dries up, so mortals lie down and do not rise again; until the heavens are no more, they will not awake or be roused out of their sleep.[11]

And, the author might have added, "Have a nice day."

It is easy for Christians to immediately address these dark realities with the story of divine suffering and redemption that lies at the heart of Christian belief. And that is indeed part of the message—God has overcome darkness and death, a victory of which we are the beneficiaries. Yet this powerful story can quickly become little more than a superficial panacea for all the darkness and loss that surrounds each of us, a truism that can blind us to an otherwise inescapable truth: *mortals die, and are laid low*. And during its short duration, human life is often filled with nothing but suffering, pain, and meaninglessness.

All sorts of responses to these dark realities, ranging from religious through philosophical and literary to political, have been offered over the centuries, responses that often conflict with each other and even more frequently fail to take the fundamental problem on squarely. Which of these

---

11. Job 14:1–2, 7, 10–12.

stories is true? More importantly, how can we know if *any* of them are true? How can we be sure that these stories are anything more than a collection of tunes human beings have written to whistle in the dark until the night overwhelms them? I submit that we cannot be sure. Yet billions of people have been willing to shape their lives, to stake their very existence at least virtually, sometimes literally, on the truth of one or more of these stories. Why? Because there is something in the human heart that has to believe them, something that has to hope. And it is that very longing and hope that is perhaps most convincing. As Simone Weil reminds us, "If we ask our Father for bread, he will not give us a stone."[12]

Magda Trocme, one of the leaders of the rescue efforts in the little French village of Le Chambon where thousands of refugees, Jewish and otherwise, were successfully hidden from the Gestapo and Vichy police during the dark years of World War II, is one of my models concerning matters of the spirit and faith. Magda's husband, Andre, was the dynamic Protestant pastor in Le Chambon; his powerful and eloquent sermons inspired his congregation to live out their faith in real time in the face of possible prison and other life-threatening dangers. Magda had no patience for theological niceties and regularly scoffed at the notion that her astounding generosity and fearless hospitality that were exemplars for her fellow villagers made her a "saint" or even morally special. She just did what needed to be done and facilitated the efforts of others to do the same, addressing every human need within her power to address no matter who the human in need happened to be. I have studied the Le Chambon phenomenon for a number of years and have used the story of this remarkable village in class many times. But it was not until recently while reading Patrick Henry's new study of the village that I encountered Magda saying anything about God. In her unpublished memoirs, now in the archives at Swarthmore College, Magda provides her definition of God:

> If there weren't somewhere a source of hope, justice, truth, and love, we would not have rooted in us the hope of justice, truth, and love that we find in every religion and every degree of civilization. It's that source that I call God.[13]

The third and final portion of Handel's *Messiah*, immediately following the "Hallelujah Chorus," begins with "I Know That My Redeemer Liveth," a

---

12. Weil, *Waiting*, 58–59.
13. Quoted in Henry, *We Only Know Men*, 40.

soaring, spectacularly beautiful soprano solo setting of the following text from Job, with a concluding sentiment from 1 Corinthians:

> I know that my redeemer liveth, and that he shall stand at the latter day upon the earth;
>
> And though worms destroy this body, yet in my flesh shall I see God.[14]
>
> For now is Christ risen from the dead, the first fruits of them that sleep.[15]

From the depths of despair, literally from the middle of a pile of ashes, Job embraces a hopeful story, that there is a transcendent and triumphant divine response to human incapacity, despair, and hopelessness. It's a wonderful story. I believe, hope, and pray that it is true. It had better be.

---

14. Job 19:25–26.
15. 1 Cor 15:20.

2

Idolatry—The Designer God Project

I am a huge college basketball fan. Actually, I am a huge Providence College Friars fan, not surprising since I have taught at Providence College, and lived in Providence for twenty-two years and counting. There's nothing like Division One college basketball—I have had two season tickets to Friars games for twenty-two years and have probably missed no more than a dozen home games (except for the semester I was in Minnesota on sabbatical). Early in our time here in Providence, I received a Friars sweatshirt for Christmas. I particularly liked it because it was a turtleneck. I like turtlenecks. They are an essential part of a professor's winter wardrobe (usually worn with a corduroy jacket, an even more indispensable sartorial item—I have five). The comfort and warmth of this sweatshirt, along with its understated "Providence Friars" on the front, made it a "must-wear" item for every home game.

This item of clothing took on even greater importance when I realized, after several home games, that the Friars had never lost a game that I attended wearing the sweatshirt. So, of course, I continued wearing it and the Friars kept winning. This continued for more than one season, until on the way to a game one evening my son Justin noted that even though I do not have an extensive wardrobe, it was not necessary to wear the same damn thing to every game (especially since I also owned a T-shirt or two with the Friars logo). I then let him in on the secret: "We have never lost a game that I attended wearing this sweatshirt." I felt that I had let my son in on one

Idolatry — The Designer God Project

of the best-kept secrets of the universe, but he simply responded, "Yes we have, Dad." I vigorously denied his claim, of course, but to no avail. "You were wearing it at the final home game last year when Pittsburgh kicked our ass, and at the game before that when we lost in overtime to Villanova!" It sucks to have someone with total recall of trivial facts in the family—I knew better than to challenge his memory, since every time I have done so in the past I have been proven wrong. Thinking back, I speculated that Jeanne must have (without my knowledge) washed the sweatshirt for the first time ever before last year's Villanova game and inadvertently washed away the secret substance that guaranteed Friars' wins.

I had been the victim of magical thinking—the identification of causal relationships between actions and events where there are no such relationships. There is a fallacy in logic describing this way of thinking with the very cool name *post hoc, ergo propter hoc*: "after this, therefore because of this." Thinking that the Friars won every game that I wore my special sweatshirt to, I concluded that they must have won *because* I wore my special sweatshirt. Avid sports fans are notoriously susceptible to magical thinking—lucky clothes, coins, and ritualistic activities from what food and beverage is consumed on game day to the path driven to the sports bar all are treated as causal links to victory. Check out Robert De Niro in the 2012 film *Silver Linings Playbook* to see it in action. But don't scoff at or feel badly for the avid sports fans. All human beings are susceptible to magical thinking, often in areas of belief and activity far more serious than sporting events.

Magical thinking is more pervasive in religious belief than any other sort. Such belief often is energized by the question of how to tap into divine power, to cultivate a relationship with what is greater than we are. From prayers said in a certain way through rosary beads to donations to charitable organizations, virtually any practice can take on the aura of being *the* way to attract God's attention, to make it most likely that the divine interest will be drawn toward my little corner of the universe. Vast numbers of books have been written concerning and dollars spent promoting the latest suggestions as to how to get God involved directly in my wishes and desires. The funny thing is that such practices and activities occasionally seem to work. I prayed in a certain way for a person to be healed, for someone else to find a job, for a favored politician to win election—and it happens. *Post hoc, ergo propter hoc.* Those who promote or invent seemingly successful techniques for gaining God's attention rise to the status of guru or spiritual giant, and everything they say, write, or do takes on special significance.

But crashing disappointment always comes and it turns out that the life of faith is not magic after all. There are as many days and weeks of slogging through an apparently empty desert of belief as there are mountaintop experiences where it seems that God has decided to channel divine energy directly through me. It turns out that whatever the divine is, it is not a slot machine, a formula to be solved, or an incantation to be performed. This is why Jesus resisted performing miracles on demand. He knew that magical thinking is powerfully seductive because it is easy, because it frees us from the challenging work of day-to-day seeking. Jesus likened the divine to the wind, which we cannot predict and which blows where and when it wants. The very air we breathe is infused with the divine. Everything is sacramental, but there are no sacred cows.

Voltaire once said that if God did not exist, it would be necessary to invent him. In truth, we invent God all the time, often with seeming disregard as to whether the God we have invented actually exists or not. In a similar vein, Anne Lamott suggests that "you can safely assume you've created God in your own image when it turns out that God hates all the same people you do."[1] So how am I, or how is any God-believer, supposed to tell whether the God I believe in exists in reality, or simply as a figment of my self-obsessed imagination? Exploring these issues with eighteen-year-olds in the classroom is always both dynamic and illuminating.

Almost every fall, one of the early reading assignments in the interdisciplinary program I teach in is the first twenty-five chapters of Genesis and the first twenty-four of Exodus. After assuring my students, many of whom are the product of twelve years of parochial school education, that no one has ever been struck dead in any of my classes for speaking honestly about their reactions to what they've read in a "sacred text," a few brave souls begin to admit that the God of these stories from the Jewish Scriptures is quite different from the God they had been taught to believe in. This God frequently seems insecure, petty, unfair, and arbitrary—what's up with that?

Last fall after a few minutes in this seminar, it occurred to me that a thought experiment was in order. I said "Okay, if you don't like the God of Genesis and Exodus, let's work for a while on what we *do* want God to be and to act like. Let's create a 'Designer God'—you get to create God from scratch. Write in your notebooks for ten minutes on the following topic:

---

1. Lamott, *Bird*, 22.

Idolatry—The Designer God Project

Any God worth believing in will have the following characteristics. Come up with three characteristics and explain why any God worth believing in would have to have them. Go."

After the writing portion of the thought experiment, the students compared notes and found that the God they had just designed individually was pretty similar from person to person. As they offered their favored divine characteristics, I wrote the list on the board:

- Forgiving
- Trustworthy
- Understanding
- Fair/Just
- Loving
- Powerful
- Dependable
- All-Knowing
- Not a micromanager

As we discussed selected characteristics on the list, a number of issues were revealed.

Fairness: The biggest problem the students had with the Old Testament God is that this is a God who plays favorites. Any God worth believing in should treat everyone the same. "Why?" I asked. "Do all of you treat everyone the same? Do you like the seven billion-plus people in the world equally? Do you even like the few dozen people that you know really well the same?" They had to admit that they didn't. "Then why do you expect God to do something that you make no attempt to do?" I wondered. After struggling for an answer, they concluded that God is God and we're not—the divine should be held to a higher standard than we are, although where that standard might come from other than from God they weren't sure.

Loving: At first, the idea was that any God worth believing in should be loving. Period. "Even mass murderers, drug dealers, and child abusers?" I asked. Well, several thought, we need to qualify this love thing a bit. God should love those who deserve it, or those who believe in God, but not everyone indiscriminately. Love that is equally spread everywhere without qualification is cheapened somehow. God's love is transactional, in other words. I do this, God responds with love.

Powerful: Omnipotence turned out to be a big one—no God worth believing in is wimpy or weak. "But God in Genesis and Exodus *is* powerful and has no problem exhibiting that power on a regular basis. And you didn't like that," I reminded them. As it turned out, Designer God should be powerful but should not be about using that power all the time. "When is it appropriate for God to use that divine power?" "Whenever I or my group is in trouble or needs something" was the most common response. So you want God to be like a 911 operator or a lifeline on *Who Wants to be a Millionaire?* That didn't sound right, but maybe so. Which led to another Designer God must-have trait.

Dependable: God needs to "be there" was the way that many students put it—"dependable" and "trustworthy." "Being there" means responsive and on call, rather than omnipresent and in your face—the students clearly were not interested in a proactive God who demanded much of them. When things are going badly, listen up and answer my prayers. When things are going well, leave me the hell alone. The students were largely in agreement when I reframed this trait as a requirement that God not be a micromanager. An overall plan for my life is fine, but I want to have a great deal of choice in terms of how I decide to find out about and pursue that plan (even freedom *not* to follow that plan if I so choose).

As we entered the last half hour of seminar, I asked everyone to take a mental step back and look at the list of Designer God characteristics that we had been discussing. Truth be told, the God we had designed looked like a combination of a non-interfering Santa Claus and my students' parents on a good day. Or the personality traits of the pleasant, vanilla God they had been taught to believe in. The question to ask, I suggested, is "What evidence is there that the God you have just designed actually exists?" Is there any evidence that these are the character traits of the divine, or are these simply a projection of what we want to believe in? A careful and clear consideration of the world we actually live in reveals that for every piece of evidence supporting the existence of Designer God, an equally obvious piece of evidence suggests either the Designer God's non-existence, or—perhaps more challenging—that whatever God is, God is something quite mysterious, exhibiting characteristics not on our list, and well outside our comfort zones. The Designer God project was a two-hour exercise in creating God in our own image. And maybe that's where most of us would like to stay. We're like the Israelites in Exodus who get the shit scared out of them when God actually talks to them directly. They are very uncomfortable with the noise, the lightning, the fire, and the obvious power. Their response? "Moses, *you* go talk to God and tell us what God wants. We can deal with you, but don't want to deal with that."[2]

The story is told that St. Augustine used to get annoyed with his students when, as he pointed toward something he wished them to consider, they focused their attention on his finger instead. More than two-and-a-half decades of teaching experience confirms the truth behind this story. The default state of students is far more likely to be "what do *you* think?" (so we can repeat it back for your reading pleasure on the next exam) rather than grasping the opportunity to look at something new with an experienced guide. The whole structure of higher education is organized around the idea that students and their parents will pay thousands of dollars per year for students to sit regularly in the presence of experts who will, in various ways, shape and mold their young charges into something useful and marketable. I spent many years of hard work and a lot of money in order to get to be one of the shapers and molders. So listen to me, and find as many ways as possible to let me know how brilliant I am on a regular basis.

But that, of course, is not how learning happens. Over the years I've come to realize that it is vitally important for me, every day in the classroom, to remember the difference between an *idol* and an *icon*. Both idols and icons are meant to be looked at, and as such must be capable of attracting attention. But attention is intended to stop at the idol—it is the final focus of the attention being paid. An icon, on the other hand, directs one's attention through to something beyond, something other than the icon itself. The idol says "Look at me!" while the icon says "Look through me at this over here." When the classroom is at its best, the energy is iconic, not idolatrous. Augustine's annoyance with his third-century–CE class arose because his students were treating him as an idol when he was trying to be an icon. "Don't look at me—look *through* me to see something greater and more interesting than any of us."

We twenty-first-century people don't tend to think a lot about the dangers of idolatry, but we should. Great philosophers in the Western tradition from Plato through Immanuel Kant to Iris Murdoch in the twentieth century have drawn the attention of anyone who would listen to the fact that by nature, human beings are incurable idolaters, more than happy to pattern themselves after someone or something else than to take responsibility

---

2. Exod 20:18–19.

for themselves. Kant goes so far as to describe the Second Commandment, "You shall not make for yourself an idol, whether in the form of anything that is in heaven above, or that is on the earth beneath, or that is in the water under the earth,"[3] as the most sublime commandment of the Jewish law. Simone Weil wrote that "We are really and truly suffering from the disease of idolatry, and it is so deeply rooted that it takes away from Christians the power to bear witness to the truth."[4] Idolatry, understood in a nonreligious way, is the powerful tendency of human beings to be satisfied with something that is a mere shadow or reflection of the real thing. We desire the good, the pure, the truth, but lack the patience and fortitude to pursue it wherever that pursuit might lead. Idolatry is the vice of premature closure, of accepting a sham for the real thing—then becoming convinced that the sham is the real thing.

The Designer God exercise my students and I engaged in together is an example of idolatry, just a bit more explicit than usual. Just as Voltaire suggested we might do, we invented God out of our preferences and desires, neglecting to include any divine characteristics that might challenge, deny, or redirect whatever we were most comfortable with. One of the most familiar texts on idolatry is the story of the golden calf from Exodus. Moses has gone to the top of the mountain to get instructions directly from God while the children of Israel remain and wait in the desert at the bottom of the mountain. Before long, they get impatient and fall back on what they know and are most comfortable with. An idol made of gold, such as the ones in Egypt where they came from, is tangible and predictable—this is something we can control. But of course it is not the real thing—not even close.[5]

There is something in the human heart that, as Iris Murdoch writes, "yearn[s] for the transcendent, for God, for something divine and good and pure,"[6] yet there is something equally powerful in us that within short order writes a job description and paints a picture of that transcendent something. Then we convince ourselves that what we just created in our own image is the real thing. The author of Hebrews suggests that it is "a fearful thing to fall into the hands of the living God."[7] Something created

3. Exod 20:4.
4. Weil, *Need*, 256.
5. Exod 32.
6. Murdoch, *Metaphysics*, 56.
7. Heb 10:31.

Idolatry—The Designer God Project

in my own image is far more predictable and manageable. The uncomfortable thing about adventuring with a real God rather than hanging out with a projection of myself is that it opens the door to continual growth and surprise and blows the doors off my comfort zone. Walking with God is like Forrest Gump's box of chocolates. You never know what you're going to get.

Certainty is a relic, an atavism, a husk we ought to have outgrown. Mystery is openness to possibility, even at the scale now implied by physics and cosmology.[8] —Marilynne Robinson

"Does God exist?" is a question that has never held much interest for me, philosophically or otherwise. I don't think any of the arguments designed to answer the question positively actually work very well; over time I have lost interest in the question almost entirely. The God whose existence is usually being wondered about when this question gets asked is a being separate and distinct from the universe, a supreme being who created the universe a long time ago. This God's résumé usually includes personality traits such as omnipotence, omniscience, and omnibenevolence; God thus described is often imagined with authoritarian and parental attributes, with all of the positive and negative baggage accompanying (unlike my students' Designer God who possessed only the positive character traits). In his recent book *Convictions*, Marcus Borg calls belief in the existence of this being "Supernatural Theism." For non-theists who deny the existence of God, it is almost always the God of Supernatural Theism whose existence is being denied; it is also this God that is the target of the impassioned attacks of "New Atheists" like Sam Harris, Richard Dawkins, and Daniel Dennett. Borg notes that when someone tells him that she or he does not believe in God, he "learned many years ago to respond, 'Tell me about the God you don't believe in.' It was always the God of supernaturalism."[9] Borg says that he stopped believing in that God when he was in his twenties (he was in his seventies when he recently passed away). I don't believe in that God either.

It isn't that I now believe in the existence of a divine being with a different resume. It's rather that "does God exist?" is the wrong question. Because the issue of God is not existential—it's not about whether there is

---

8. Robinson, *When I Was*, 197.
9. Borg, *Convictions*, 48.

another being out there in addition to the universe, another item in the list of "stuff that exists." Rather, the issue of God is experiential. The psalmist says "taste and see that the Lord is good,"[10] and tasting and seeing are not arguments, rationalizations, or proofs. The divine, the sacred is real in my life as an element of experience, not as a hypothetical being who may or may not exist and whom we can only believe in.

Many recent thinkers call this orientation "mysticism," and refer to experiences that might be described as "mystical" that helped bring them to this experiential conclusion. This makes sense because, at a certain point, mystics in all faiths realize that the myths and doctrines of their tradition are only human-made; they are simply "pointers" to a transcendence that cannot be expressed in normal words and concepts. Mysticism conceived in this way is the refusal to deny the existence of the transcendent, accompanied by the refusal to assume that one understands what the transcendent is in any full sense. Drawn between the poles of the human need for certainty and closure and the open-ended magnetic attraction of the transcendent, the mystic refuses to "fill in the blanks." I possess few of the traits of the stereotypical mystic (levitation, ability to go long periods of time without food, a certain glazed countenance), but I do resonate with Lawrence Kushner's definition of a "mystic" in *Kabbalah: A Love Story*.

> A mystic is anyone who has the gnawing suspicion that the apparent discord, brokenness, contradictions, and discontinuities that assault us every day might conceal a hidden unity.[11]

Suspicion is a well-chosen term, because a reorientation from Supernatural Theism to what might be called Mystical Theism (if one needs a title) is difficult to talk about and impossible to provide convincing arguments for. Words fail me, although I keep trying to find them. More often than not I fall back on the evidence of a "changed life" and "come and see," finding strength in the fact that those who have also experienced the sacred and have not just thought about it resonate with me on a level deeper than words. They just "know" what I am trying to convey. Not the usual path toward verification for a philosopher, but it works very well for human beings.

What might Mystical Theism say about the fractured and disjointed world in which we live? Trying to square such a world with the God of

---

10. Ps 34:8.
11. Kushner, *Kabbalah*, 54.

Idolatry—The Designer God Project

Supernatural Theism gives rise to the problem of evil, perhaps the most intractable philosophical/theological problem of all: why does a God with this résumé allow the world to be in the state it is in? But as Kushner suggests, there is a different orientation available.

> If you are a mystic, saying you believe in God means that you have an abiding suspicion that everything is a manifestation of God, and no matter how horrific it might be, it is still, somehow, filled with holiness.[12]

The only evidence for that is experiential, and even such experience is iffy and enigmatic. I have not had the "road to Damascus" sorts of experiences that have changed the lives of many. My reorientation has been more gradual, which for me means it is likely to have the permanence that a "once for all" experience might lack. As I sat for many weeks in daily prayer with Benedictine monks several years ago, the reorientation began as I noticed a slow opening of peaceful spaces inside and a new way of seeing what is around me. This does not conflict with my intellect, my mind, or my philosophy—it holds it in place.

---

12. Ibid., 125.

3

Change—Living with Provisional Faith

In order to find Truth, you must have an unremitting readiness to admit you may be wrong.[1] —Joan Chittister

Starting college at age eighteen, 3,000 miles away from home, would have been daunting under other circumstances. But as I watched my father drive away from the Santa Fe campus of St. John's College in August of 1974 after our week-long drive from northern Vermont, a trip that delivered me to my freshman year at the only college I ever applied to with a "great books" curriculum designed for pointy-headed geeks like me, I was inwardly rejoicing. "I'll be staying close by in the area for a few days in case you change your mind," Dad promised through the open driver's-side window after he shut the door, obviously looking for signs of tears in my eyes. "Okay," I said. *Fat chance of that happening*, I thought. This was a chance for me to reinvent myself amongst people who knew nothing of my history and baggage that often felt like the burden Christian lugged around on his back for the majority of John Bunyan's *The Pilgrim's Progress*.

No one in college knew about how tough my adolescent years in school had been, with few friends and as the frequent target of ridicule for reasons ranging from my close-to-straight-A academic performance to my

---

1. Chittister, *Wisdom Distilled*, 135.

concert pianist aspirations to my general incompetence at team sports to my raging introversion. Come to think of it, though, probably most of my fellow new freshmen had been similar targets for similar reasons in their junior high and high school experiences. Most importantly, no one here knew that I was a preacher's kid, that I had been steeped in a particular version of conservative Protestantism since infancy, or that I had spent the last academic year, after graduating from high school at age sixteen, as a student at the tiny Bible school my father was president of because everyone agreed (without asking me) that barely seventeen was too early to enter college. As far as I was concerned, I would be perfectly happy to never darken the door of a church again. I was starting over.

There is, of course, only a certain amount of starting over from scratch that any human being, even an eighteen-year-old, can do. But my plan worked in a number of ways and I felt more at home and comfortable in my own skin in college than I ever had. Then ,during the fall semester of my sophomore year, our seminar text for several weeks was the Old Testament. I was raised on Bible stories, forced to memorize large portions of Scripture from age five all the way through high school, but this was the first time I ever had the opportunity to read the Bible as literature rather than as "God's word," in an academic seminar context rather than in church. I was psyched, and I thoroughly enjoyed every moment of this strange secular and sacred brew. But then one evening after seminar, the guy in the dorm room next to mine, who was also in my seminar, popped his head in the door. "You're a Christian, aren't you?" John asked. His tone was not accusatory; he was just seeking information. Apparently it was becoming increasingly clear to my seminar mates that I knew a hell of a lot more about the Bible than they did. My reinvention efforts were suddenly at risk.

It was one of those moments such as one occasionally encounters in movies or TV shows—time stood still as I stepped out of myself and considered how to get out of this. "What the fuck are you talking about, dude?" was one possibility, but I wasn't feeling it. "Yes indeed, I am a born-again Christian. You want to be one too?" was another, but I wasn't feeling that either (if I ever had). In a classic case of "How do I know what I'm thinking until I hear myself say it?" I finally said "Yes I am, and it works for me. But if you have anything that works better, I want to hear about it." I liked that answer. It marginally committed me to something (although in a way that would have made the folks back home cringe), but didn't make me sound like a Bible-thumping fanatic. I had not overtly rejected my faith; instead I sort of turned it into a matter of preference or taste. All the time sounding open-minded, liberal, and uninterested in talking about it any further. Not bad, and it worked. I don't recall that John, or anyone else, ever asked me about being a Christian again.

I was reminded of this encounter recently as I read *Choose Life*, a collection of sermons delivered by Rowan Williams on Christmas and Easter at Canterbury Cathedral during his ten-year tenure as Archbishop of Canterbury. In "The Hidden Seed of Glory," his 2009 Easter sermon, Williams begins by describing how often interviewers ask him questions such as "How do you *know* God exists?" or "How do you *know* Christian faith is true?" There are, the archbishop continues, two tempting ways for a person claiming to be a Christian to respond, both problematic. The first is what Williams calls "the apologetic shuffle"—"Of course I don't really *know*; this is just the truth as it appears to me and I may be wrong." The second is "the confident offer to prove it all"—"here are the philosophical arguments, here is the historical evidence, now what's the problem?"[2]

This caught my attention, because although I've never been tempted to go the "confident offer" route (the philosopher in me knows *that* won't work), what I told my friend concerning my Christianity over forty years ago was a version of Williams's "apologetic shuffle." Truth be told, I've been apologetically shuffling concerning my faith for just about all of the forty years since on the rare occasions in which I was not able to hide it. I often urge my students, who tend to have an unwarranted and unearned dogmatism about whatever it is that they believe, to get in the habit of tacking on to the end of belief claims something like "this is what I believe, but I have a lot to learn," or "this is what I believe, but I might be wrong." The problem with saying that concerning one's faith, as Rowan Williams points out, is that "it reduces faith to opinion and shrinks the scale of what you are trying to talk about to the dimensions of your own mind and preferences."[3] So if I believe that my Christian faith is more than a matter of subjective personal preference, and also know that my faith cannot be proven true on the basis of factual evidence and logical argumentation, what options remain? Is there a navigable path of faith between the Scylla of dogmatism and the Charybdis of subjectivity?

I have slowly become aware of the best, and perhaps only, way to communicate about my faith only recently. Williams expresses it simply

2. Williams, *Choose Life*, 171.
3. Ibid.

Change—Living with Provisional Faith

and beautifully. "Resurrection has started. How do we know? Not by working it out and adopting it as a well-founded opinion, not by getting all the arguments straight, but because we are dimly aware of something having changed around us."[4] And this change cannot be simply talked about—it can only be lived. A changed life is the only evidence. During my last sabbatical, as slow and incremental changes were happening internally, for the first time my faith was becoming real in a way that transcended both personal preference and logical analysis.

> We need to hear what is so often the question that's *really* being asked when people say, "How do you know?" And perhaps the only response that is fully adequate, fully in tune with the biblical witness to the resurrection, is to say simply, "Are you hungry? Here is food."[5]

I just don't trust people who are convinced that they know the truth.[6]
—Marcus Borg

A couple of summers ago the regular cycle of Sunday readings walked us through the familiar and fascinating stories of the patriarchs in Genesis and the dramatic escape of the children of Israel from Egyptian bondage in Exodus. Once free from Egypt, the Israelites find themselves deep in a desert; Moses is up on Mount Sinai hanging out while God writes the Ten Commandments and everyone else figures he's never coming back. So they build the golden calf, start a minor orgy, and you know how that worked out. Moses is pissed; God is even more pissed. "Jesus Christ!" God yells (he forgot what part of the Bible he was in for a moment). "I've had enough of these clowns! Stand back, Moses, while I wipe them all out. Then I'll start over again with a new bunch of people beginning with you, sort of like I did with Noah in the previous book." Moses points out that this would make God look bad, given that he put so much effort and creative thought—from plagues to parting a sea—into getting these people out of slavery, only to kill them in the desert. God's response to Moses's point is both astounding

---

4. Ibid., 173.
5. Ibid., 179.
6. Borg, *Putting Away*, 265.

and liberating: "And the Lord changed His mind."[7] The implications are unlimited.

In spite of knowing that change is inevitable, human beings spend a massive amount of time and energy trying to avoid it. Often this avoidance is described as "the search for truth." Truth is a slippery business, but everyone seems to have something to say about it. For instance, Jesus is memorably reported as having said that "you will know the truth, and the truth will set you free."[8] This is one of the many things I wish Jesus had never said, not because I think it is wrong but rather because it has been subject to all sorts of misinterpretation and coopted by all sorts of agendas. For instance, many suggest that the "truth" Jesus is referring to is actually the "Truth." The capital letter makes all the difference, as it signifies that the person making the proposal believes in *absolute* Truth. Absolute Truths are universal, fixed, inflexible, and not subject to the subjective preferences of mere mortals such as ourselves. This sounds attractive—such Truths, if they exist, would provide an indispensable touchstone for adjudicating conflicts between mere *truths*, items which often are mere projections of our own preferences and interests that we seek to implement to the greatest extent our power and influence allows.

There are at least two problems with the idea of absolute Truths. First, many agree that such Truths exist but few agree on what they actually are. It may be that absolutes do exist, but it may also be that discovering their content is far more difficult and complicated than many "True believers" want to admit. This leads to the second problem—true believers tend to cut corners in the search process, adopting what very well may be just provisional as if it is an absolute, then beating others over the heads, either virtually or actually, with their Truth pretenders. I recently spent a semester with my students in two different courses studying the limitless ways in which human beings have used Truths they claim to be in possession of—religious, political, what have you—to justify violence against and killing of fellow human beings who happen to embrace different and incompatible Truths. The Crusades, various wars of religion, the Nazis—virtually *any* truth claim can be dressed up as a Truth and used as a weapon of mass destruction. The best comment on this dynamic I ever read came from the author of a letter to the editor in the local newspaper a number of years ago: "Pursue the truth, and run like hell from anyone who claims to have it."

7. Exod 32:14.
8. John 8:32.

The fact of the matter concerning truth was clearly expressed by one of my colloquium students who wrote the following in her intellectual notebook: "The truth will not set you free, but it will definitely mess your life up." This is because the truth about the truth for human beings is that it is a process rather than a thing. The truth is more like a continuing creative act than a treasure hunt that will hopefully stumble into the pot of gold at the end of an evanescent rainbow. The truth, in other words, is something that we make. This is not a surprise, because as a matter of fact *all* ways of seeing reality are human constructions. Truth is not an exception. Everything we believe is a product of a complex filtering and organizing process through any number of filters, from genetic to experiential. Truth is a relative business—relative to each human being since each of our filters are uniquely ours.

This does not mean, however, that anything goes. It does not mean that we simply get to make truth up as we go along, as those who fear the ogre "relativism" would claim. Jesus said something else about truth that is directly applicable—"I am the way, the truth, and the life."[9] Truth is not something we find at the end of a search—it is in fact the search itself, a search that in many traditions is connected directly to a way of life, a person. The "I am the way" alternative to self-interest and power is that truth is a divine process in which we participate; our participation is energized positively by the things for which we hope and the things which we love.

Faith in God is, finally, faith in change.[10] —Christian Wiman

I love historical fiction; the genre doesn't get any better than when in the hands of Hilary Mantel. Mantel wrote a trilogy immersing readers in the world of Henry VIII as seen through the eyes of his consigliere Thomas Cromwell. Early in *Wolf Hall*, the first volume in the trilogy, Thomas Cromwell flashes back to when he was a young star in Cardinal Wolsey's orbit, a firmament containing another, brighter star—Thomas More—who in Mantel's treatment becomes one of Cromwell's opponents and competitors for the attention of the great and powerful. Cromwell reveals a fundamental difference between him and More that raises issues transcending this particular story:

9. John 14:6.
10. Wiman, *Bright Abyss*, 26.

> He [Cromwell] never sees More . . . without wanting to ask him, what's wrong with you? Or what's wrong with me? Why does everything you know, and everything you've learned, confirm you in what you believed before? Whereas in my case, what I grew up with, and what I thought I believed, is chipped away a little and a little, a fragment then a piece and then a piece more. With every month that passes, the corners are knocked off the certainties of this world: and the next world too. Show me where it says, in the Bible, "purgatory." Show me where it says "relics, monks, nuns." Show me where it says "Pope."[11]

Or, I might add, show me where it says "liturgy" or "dogma" or any number of other things that are staples of Christian tradition and practice even outside Catholicism. I have no idea whether Mantel's characterization of Cromwell and More is historically accurate, but I am so strongly aligned by nature with fictional Cromwell in this passage that I share his utter astonishment with the fictional Mores among us.

Wolf Hall is set during the early decades of the sixteenth century when the revolutionary impact of the Protestant Reformation is already making itself known in England. Thomas More is the epitome of religious certainty, imagined by Mantel as a vigorous, devout, hair-shirt-wearing and frequently inflexible defender of Catholic orthodoxy. Although Cromwell rises to influence as the right-hand man of the powerful Cardinal Wolsey, he is far more comfortable with situational flexibility than with preestablished beliefs and principles. When Wolsey falls from grace because of his failure to facilitate the king's desire to divorce Catherine of Aragon in order to marry Anne Boleyn, Cromwell's ability to quickly adjust to changing circumstances and maneuver creatively brings him into the king's inner circle. But he always keeps the Mores of his world in view, simultaneously envious and wary of anyone's unflinching commitment to inflexible principle.

I frequently find myself inadvertently dividing my fellow human beings into various either/or categories (introvert/extrovert, high-maintenance/low-maintenance, Platonic/Aristotelian, hedgehog/fox, and more); Cromwell/More is another important distinction, especially when religious belief is under discussion. The older I get, the more Cromwellian I become, finding that even my most fixed beliefs not only are regularly under scrutiny, but that constant adjustment and change is a symptom of a healthy faith. Christian Wiman writes that this "is why every single expression of

---

11. Mantel, *Wolf Hall*, 36.

Change—Living with Provisional Faith

faith is provisional—because life carries us always forward to a place where the faith we'd fought so hard to articulate to ourselves must now be reformulated, and because faith in God is, finally, faith in change."[12] The divine cannot be contained within or reduced to formulas or rigid doctrines, no matter how uncomfortable that makes us. I agree with Susan Monk Kidd, who writes that "people who want life hammered down into tight, legalistic certainties seem to me to be the people most insecure inside. Frankly, the folks who frighten me the most are those who are dead certain about everything, who have all the answers and no questions."[13]

I am frequently reminded in a number of ways by various Mores that a Cromwellian embrace of change is dangerous in that it leads to the brink of the worst of all abysses, a relativistic world with no absolutes and no fixed points. I admit that it can be disconcerting to find that one's most reliable cornerstones have crumbled or shifted, but I prefer to seek stability in commitment rather than in content. Within the well-defined banks of commitment to what is greater than us, the river of faith sometimes flows swiftly, sometimes pools stagnantly, and always offers the opportunity to explore uncharted waters. The terrain of commitment looks very different from various vantage points, and in my experience seldom provides confirmation of what I have believed in the past without change and without remainder.

The opposite of faith is not doubt, but certainty.[14] —Anne Lamott

Michel de Montaigne's world was filled with religious fervor and piety. It was also filled with hatred and violence. Sixteenth-century France was not a pretty place—in the aftermath of the Protestant Reformation, Christians were killing each other with regularity and abandon, all in the name of Christ. Catholics and Protestants each were certain that they were right; energized by such certainty, each was willing to kill the other in the name of truth and right belief.

Michel was an upper-class landowner and occasional politician—he was mayor of Bordeaux for two terms as well as a trusted royal diplomat and liaison. Sensitive and melancholy by nature, Montaigne was appalled by the violence that was tearing his country, his town, his neighborhood,

---

12. Wiman, *Bright Abyss*, 26.
13. Kidd, *When the Heart*, 158.
14. Lamott, *Plan B*, 256.

even his own family apart. Accordingly, in his middle years he did what any introverted, sensitive, melancholy guy would have done. He withdrew to his turret library in the small castle on his family estate and wrote—for the rest of his life. His finely honed powers of observation fueled his creative energies, with thousands of words spilling out onto the page often more quickly than he could think. The result, Montaigne's *Essais*, consists of fascinating and brilliant bite-sized essays on every topic imaginable, from cannibals and sexual preferences to Michel's favorite food, his kidney stones, and his cat. In the midst of this loosely organized jumble of creativity and insight, Michel frequently sounds like Rodney King in the midst of the Los Angeles riots—"Can't we all get along?"

Montaigne writes that "there is no hostility so extreme as that of the Christian. Our zeal works marvels when it seconds our inclination toward hatred, cruelty, ambition, greed, slander, and rebellion."[15] This was the world in which he lived. Michel's antidote? Let's stop claiming to be certain about what we believe and try some healthy doubt and skepticism on for size. Certainty is vastly overrated and is frequently dangerous, especially when claimed in matters that are far beyond the reach of human capacities. Montaigne is convinced that for the most part, human beings are not designed for the rarified air of certainty. He directly challenges those who "claim to know the frontiers and bounds of the will of God," observing that "there is nothing in the whole world madder than bringing such matters down to the measure of our own capacities."[16] Is there anything more ludicrous, he asks, than our propensity to believe most firmly that which we know least about and to be most sure of ourselves when we are furthest from what we can verify? Human beings claiming certainty about the will and nature of God would be humorous, and Michel often presents it that way, were it not that such claims are often the basis for the worst of what human beings are capable of, including prejudice, violence, and killing. Even as we seek preposterously to elevate ourselves to the level of the divine, Montaigne reminds us that we remain rooted in our humanity. "There is no use our mounting on stilts, for on stilts we must still walk on our own legs. And on the loftiest throne in the world we are still sitting only on our own ass."[17]

Because of his willingness to embrace messiness and uncertainty as part of the human experience, because of his willingness to call chaos what

---

15. Montaigne, *Apology*, 6.
16. Montaigne, *Essays*, 75.
17. Ibid., 426.

Change—Living with Provisional Faith

it is and not something else, Montaigne is one of my heroes. And so, for similar reasons, is a much maligned member of Jesus' disciple entourage—Thomas. "Doubting Thomas," as he almost always is described, occupies a unique place in the line-up of disciples. He's the one who wouldn't believe that Jesus had risen, wouldn't believe secondhand reports from eye witnesses, until he saw Jesus himself, until he saw the wounds in his hands, feet, and side. Thomas was always brought to our attention in Sunday school as someone *not* to be like; indeed, Jesus' putdown of Thomas after Thomas finally believes—"Blessed are those who have not seen and yet have come to believe"[18]—provides us 2,000 years later with something to be proud of. *We*, not having seen, are the blessed ones while *Thomas* (the loser) gets in by the skin of his teeth.

But what if Thomas is a model of how to approach the spiritual life? We don't know much about Thomas apart from this story; he is included in the list of disciples in the first three gospels, but John is the only Gospel in which Thomas makes an actual appearance. He's not one of the inner circle, but occasionally makes appropriate comments and asks good questions. In John's account of the resurrection and its aftermath, we find the disciples, minus Thomas, hiding in a room with the doors locked "for fear of the Jews."[19] Peter and John have already seen the empty tomb, but there is an atmosphere of confusion, uncertainty, and fear in the room. Jesus appears to them, and all uncertainty vanishes. But Thomas was not there.

Where was he? Perhaps he wasn't as afraid as the other disciples and was out and about on that first day of the week, as were the women who first saw the empty tomb. Perhaps he was on a food run for the rest of the disciples who were too frightened to emerge from their safe house. But he misses the big event. When the other disciples report that "we have seen the Lord," Thomas's response places him forever in the disciples' hall of shame: "Unless I see the mark of the nails in his hands, and put my finger in the mark of the nails and my hand in his side, I will not believe."[20]

Fair enough, I say. Remember that the other disciples did not believe until Jesus appeared to them. The disciples on the road to Emmaus did not recognize that Jesus was with them until he emerged from the pages of the prophecies that he was pontificating about and broke bread with them. Why should Thomas not be cut the same slack? Embedded in the middle

18. John 20:29.
19. John 20:19.
20. John 20:24.

of this misunderstood story is a fundamental truth: a true encounter with the divine is never second hand. Hearing about someone else's experiences, trying to find God through the haze of various religious and doctrinal filters, is not a replacement for the real thing. Doubt and uncertainty are central threads in the human fabric and play a fundamental role in belief. Unfounded claims of certainty undermine this. Don't believe on the cheap. Better to remain uncertain and in doubt one's whole life, doggedly tracking what glimmers of light one sees, than to settle for a cheap knock-off or a counterfeit. As Annie Dillard writes, "Doubt and dedication often go hand in hand."[21] Thomas's—and Michel's—insight is captured well by Anne Lamott:

> The opposite of faith is not doubt, but certainty. Certainty is missing the point entirely. Faith includes noticing the mess, the emptiness and discomfort, and letting it be there until some light returns.[22]

Thomas was right. We should save "My Lord and my God"[23] for the real thing.

---

21. Dillard, *For the Time*, 146.
22. Lamott, *Plan B*, 256.
23. John 20:28.

4

Attentiveness—There It Is

Rainer Maria Rilke once said of Paul Cezanne that the great impressionist artist did not paint "I like it," he painted "There it is."[1] There is an important analogy here that extends beyond the world of art. One way of thinking about the moral life is that it involves learning how to get out of the way of my own line of vision in order to truly see the existence of something else, a natural object, a person in need. How do I learn to engage things as they are rather than as I wish them to be, to remember that I am not, after all, the center of the universe? How do I keep from stifling the beauty and promise of a day by wrapping it in what Iris Murdoch calls "the anxious avaricious tentacles of the self"?[2]

At a writer's workshop several summers ago one of the writing coaches suggested that we ask ourselves the following question every time we sit down to write: "With *Middlemarch* and *Pilgrim at Tinker Creek* in the world, why would anyone be interested in *this*?" Over the twenty years or so since I read *Pilgrim at Tinker Creek* for the first time, I have occasionally mentioned how it has influenced me to friends whose opinions I highly respect. More often than not, my friend has replied that she read it years ago and didn't finish it, or he confesses that "I just don't get it." One said "I didn't like it much when I read it, but I've never been able to forget it." I understand these reactions—Annie Dillard's 1974 Pulitzer Prize winner

---

1. Quoted in Murdoch, *Existentialists*, 348.
2. Ibid.

is odd, quirky, eclectic, and one-of-a-kind. And it has helped me to see the world around me and myself differently.

Annie Dillard is an intense observer of details, capable of seeing things that escape the notice of just about everyone. She finds worlds of complexity and interest in the tiniest matters—I often think of Dr. Seuss's *Horton Hears a Who* when I read Dillard. But I have encountered skilled natural observers before—what makes Dillard different is that she invites the reader into a new kind of seeing altogether. Given, as she writes, that most of us "waste most of our energy just by spending every waking minute saying hello to ourselves,"[3] how do we learn to get out of the way and see what is actually there instead of what we expect to see?

> There is another kind of seeing, which involves a letting go. When I see this way I sway transfixed and emptied. The difference between the two ways of seeing is the difference between walking with and without a camera. When I walk with a camera I walk from shot to shot, reading the light on a calibrated meter. When I walk without a camera, my own shutter opens, and the moment's light prints on my own silver gut. When I see this second way I am above all an unscrupulous observer.[4]

When I remember to get out of my own way, *Pilgrim at Tinker Creek* serves as a standard for me, a standard of how to see differently. This theme of learning how to truly see weaves through many of the texts that have influenced me over the past several years—Annie Dillard was the first to introduce me to it.

> The secret of seeing is, then, the pearl of great price.... But although the pearl may be found, it may not be sought. The literature of illumination reveals this above all: although it comes to those who wait for it, it is always, even to the most practiced and adept, a gift and a total surprise.[5]

Almost every Sunday during the months I spent on sabbatical a few years ago in Minnesota, I saw a canine in church—I didn't know the dog's name, but it looked like a Ralph. I learned several months later that the dog is a female named Caritas, but in my imagination she still is Ralph. Ralph was in church because she was a service dog—now enjoying retirement—for a

3. Dillard, *Pilgrim*, 200.
4. Ibid., 33.
5. Ibid., 35.

Attentiveness—There It Is

regular parishioner who is profoundly deaf. She sat at the end of the front row so she could read the lips of the celebrant, while Ralph laid next to her, usually with her back half hanging out into the aisle. Ralph is a mutt, with a good deal of some sort of terrier, weighing probably no more than twenty-five or thirty pounds.

A lifelong cat lover, I've gained a much greater appreciation for dogs over the past several years after marrying a dog fanatic and, more recently, being unexpectedly adopted by a dachshund as her pet human. Ralph looked as if she would love to have a pat on the head or a belly rub, but I know better—don't mess with a service dog while she's on the clock. But just in case I, or anyone else within range, happened to have a hard time resisting the dog-lover's urge to touch every dog, Ralph was more in-your-face than most service dogs. She wore a vest that, on its back, said "Service dog on duty. Do not pet."

"Look—don't touch." This used to be my mother's automatic command every time we walked into a store of any sort, from grocery to hardware to department. Every parent worth the job description has this directive in her or his repertoire, knowing that pre-civilized human beings are inveterate grabbers. Hannah Arendt is reported to have said that the world is invaded by millions of tiny barbarians every year—these barbarians are called children. Absolutely true, and "Look, don't touch" is one of the earliest and best tools to use for domestication purposes. In truth, though, the temptation to look and grab, rather than simply to look, is one that none of us ever truly overcomes. As soon as we see something, we want to possess it and make it ours.

Exhibit A is a familiar story from Luke's gospel.[6] Jesus is worn out by the crowds and takes his best buddies, Peter, James, and John, with him to the top of a mountain for a break. While there, he is transfigured with Elijah and Moses, looking like a great laundry detergent ad. According to another version of the story, "His clothes became dazzling white, such as no one on earth could bleach them."[7] Peter blurts out, "Let us put up three dwellings—one for you, one for Moses, and one for Elijah." Why does he make such a random suggestion? Luke tells us—"He did not know what he was saying." Far be it from Peter to say nothing when he doesn't know what to say, to look and attend to what's going on in silence and awe, or simply to say "Whoa!" or "Holy shit!" or "I'm scared!" or "I don't get it." No, he has to

6. Luke 9:28–36.
7. Mark 9:3.

nail it down, organize it, put walls around it, and either sell tickets or write up a doctrinal statement and confession of faith. The voice from heaven makes it clear what Peter *should* be doing. "This is my Son, my Chosen; *listen to him.*"

Scripture makes it clear that there is a time to look and a time to touch—and don't confuse the two. In Second Samuel, the newly crowned King David leads the army of Israel against the Philistines and recaptures the ark of the covenant.[8] They place the ark on an oxen-drawn cart and head back to Jerusalem in a parade complete with singing and musical instruments, led by David dancing in his underwear. The oxen step in a pothole and stumble, the ark starts tipping off of the cart, and some poor guy named Uzzah makes the horrible mistake of assuming that he should put his hand on the ark to steady it, because maybe God would just as soon not see the ark lying on its side in the mud. God strikes Uzzah dead on the spot for his efforts. "Look, don't touch." As a kid I thought God's treatment of Uzzah to be a disproportionate response and grossly unfair, and I still do, but as Jeanne would say, "It is what it is." And in John 20, the resurrected Jesus says to Mary Magdalene "Touch me not,"[9] exactly what it would have said on Ralph's vest if she spoke in King James English.

As a native New Englander, one of my all-time favorite stories is Nathaniel Hawthorne's "The Great Stone Face." It's the story of a boy named Ernest who lives in a New Hampshire valley; on the perpendicular side of a nearby mountain hang some immense rocks which, when viewed from the proper angle and distance, closely resembled the features of a human face. The valley is Franconia Notch in the middle of the White Mountains, only forty miles or so from where I grew up. I have only driven through Franconia Notch once in the ten years since the Old Man of the Mountain fell off his cliff after many attempts to shore him up in various sorts of ways. It isn't the same.

According to Hawthorne's story, there is a legend in the valley that someday "a child should be born hereabouts, who is destined to become the greatest and noblest personage of his time, and whose countenance, in manhood, should bear an exact resemblance to the Great Stone Face."[10] Ernest, who gazes daily with love and awe at the Great Stone Face, spends his whole life as a simple laborer in the valley. Occasionally a rumor would

---

8. 2 Sam 6:1–7.

9. John 20:17 KJV.

10. Hawthorne, *Great Stone Face*, 3.

arise that the man resembling the Great Stone Face has appeared in town, but each candidate—a wealthy miser, a vain general, a pompous politician—turned out to be a fraud. As the years pass and Ernest becomes an old man, he is loved by his neighbors and family but sadly concludes that the legend will not come true in his lifetime. Then one day as he talks simply and clearly on his front porch with a number of his friends about matters important to all of them, the setting sun strikes Ernest's face and someone sitting next to him exclaims "Behold! Behold! Ernest is himself the likeness of the Great Stone Face!"[11] He had become what he had spent his life lovingly looking at.

Iris Murdoch writes that "man is a creature who makes pictures of himself and then comes to resemble the picture."[12] And the pictures we make will be fashioned from what we are looking at and what we see most clearly. What are you looking at?

In the 1991 movie *City Slickers*, Billy Crystal plays New York executive Mitch Robbins, whose hassled life is wearing negatively on his work, his marriage, and his friendships. At thirty-nine years old he finds himself deep in a midlife crisis. For his birthday, his two best buddies purchase a two-week vacation for the three of them at a dude ranch in New Mexico to participate in a dude cattle drive. The tough-as-nails trail boss, Curly, played to great effect by Jack Palance, is an enigma to Mitch from day one—Curly is silent, curmudgeonly, skilled at his job, self-assured, and clearly in possession of information that Mitch badly needs. One day while rounding up strays, Mitch asks, "Curly, what is the secret of life?" Curly holds one finger up.

"This."

"Your finger?"

"One thing. Just one thing. You stick to that and everything else don't mean shit."

"That's great, but what's the one thing?"

"That's what you've gotta figure out."

One thing. Finding out what that one thing is might be the point of anyone's life, but that's a pretty big task. One New Year's Day I asked myself "What is the one thing that I resolve to do in this coming year that will be

11. Ibid., 31.
12. Murdoch, *Existentialists*, 75.

good for the inner me, for my soul?" I resolved that in 2015 I would be a more reverent person.

Reverence is not a concept that is particularly in favor in Western culture—it probably hasn't been for decades. The term is almost always used in religious contexts, especially during the holiday season that had just ended. The shepherds and wise men gaze reverently upon the Christ child, Mary listens reverently as the angel tells her that her world is about to be turned upside down, the stable animals chew their hay reverently as they observe Mary reverently giving birth to Jesus while Joseph reverently boils water and finds some swaddling clothes. I suppose that sort of faux holiness has its place (maybe), but that's not what I have in mind.

The sort of reverence I resolved to cultivate is more like Moses's reaction to the burning bush in Exodus. As he is taking care of his father-in-law Jethro's flocks one day, he notices something weird out of the corner of his eye—a bush that is on fire but is not being burnt up. He could have thought "that's weird" and kept on going. He could have made a mental note to check back later when he wasn't so busy. He could have Googled "burning bush" on his tablet after dinner with Zipporah and the kids when he had a few minutes of down time. But he didn't. Instead, he said "I must turn aside and look at this great sight, and see why the bush is not burned up."[13] Loose translation—"Holy shit! What the hell is that?" Moses was willing to interrupt his busy day to take a look at something outside his usual frame of reference. Reverence begins with the ability to *see* in a different way, to *notice* what's going on outside the boundaries of my agenda, to *be attentive* to even the most mundane items and events that cross my path. Most importantly, reverence is cultivated by an increasing awareness that everything is important in its own right.

Human beings are naturally acquisitive and devouring creatures—we are seldom willing to let things be as they are. If X is attractive, I want to buy it. If Y looks useful, I want to consume it. We turn these manic energies on the world around us and on each other on a regular basis. But not everything is here for my use and pleasure. The importance of what I encounter during a given day is not to be judged according to how important it is to me. So in practical terms, what does reverence amount to? At the very least, it means giving each task, person, and event in my life my undivided attention. Accordingly, I resolved to ask myself this question frequently in the following weeks and months: *is what you are doing worthy of your*

---

13. Exod 3:3.

Attentiveness—There It Is

undivided attention? And if the answer is "yes," then the follow-up question is, *then why are you not giving it your undivided attention?* Learning to give my undivided attention to each thing as I encounter it is the first step in recognizing the value inherent in even the tiniest and most insignificant part of reality. Moses took the time to check out something unusual and found out that he was standing on holy ground. And so are we. All the time.

I put my New Year's resolution to the test the following weekend. As I thought about what reverence might mean outside the confines of its usual religious implications, I kept circling back to a negative definition: Reverence is the opposite of multitasking. Sitting in our little library room before dawn on the first Saturday of the year, I wondered "What is the thing most likely to suck me into multitasking?" The answer was obvious—my beloved Surface II tablet, recharged and waiting for my use, laying on the bottom shelf of the table next to my chair. What if I tried to spend twenty-four hours without turning my tablet (or either of the other laptops in the house) on? What if I lived in a "tablet-free" zone for twenty-four hours?

Immediately a swarm of questions and concerns swept over me like locusts over Egypt:

1. But what if I want to work on some essays today?
2. What if a response to one or more of the cosmically important emails I sent out yesterday comes in today?
3. How am I going to be able to track how my blog numbers are doing?
4. I was going to finish the syllabus for my upcoming Philosophy of the Human Person class today.
5. Should I tell Jeanne what I'm doing?
6. Would using my cell phone count as a violation of "no computer"?
7. How am I going to print off the essay I wrote yesterday that I'll be using at our seminar tomorrow after church?
8. Most importantly, how am I going to find out when the Friars basketball game this afternoon is?

As the above concerns arose within five minutes of my declaring the day "computer free," I scribbled them down on a yellow pad of paper. Which immediately answered concerns #1 and #4 above—there is a remarkable invention, almost as amazing as tablets, called "paper," upon which one can record one's most profound thoughts even when no computer is available.

I managed to write a new essay that Saturday; I had forgotten how horrible my handwriting is.

I did tell Jeanne what I was up to as soon as she arose because I needed her wisdom concerning #6. Does my computer sabbatical apply to my phone? "Yes it does," she immediately said, "since you use your phone like a computer instead of a phone." True enough. I hate getting phone calls, but love checking my emails and blog numbers on my phone. Which focused my attention on #2 and #3. On Sunday morning I found out that although about twenty-five emails came in on Saturday, none of them were the responses I was looking for; I deleted all but two of the twenty-five without even reading them. Maybe my emails aren't as cosmically important as I thought.

Not checking my blog numbers was a big problem, since I have become convinced that the number of times people visit my blog during a given day is directly proportional to the number of times I check my blog numbers. And guess what? That Saturday was my worst blog activity day in close to a year—obviously because I didn't check the numbers all day. By the way, I found out when the Friars basketball game was by remembering that I had a calendar in my backpack with all of the college sports events for the year. I shouldn't have bothered. They lost.

Against all odds, I made it through the day without turning a computer on or messing with my phone. Instead I took down the Christmas tree, wrote a new essay, finished the book I was reading, listened to the Friars lose on the radio, watched a bunch of TV (only some of it worth the time), and ate more than usual. But the evidence of baby steps in reverence was there. For instance, I am in the habit of marking the chapters of any book I am reading that I especially like or find insightful in the book's Table of Contents. Was it a coincidence that three of my four favorite chapters in the book I finished on computer sabbatical Saturday are chapters that I read without tablet interruption that morning? And when Jeanne told me early in the evening on Saturday that I looked "extremely content" sitting in my chair in the living room, I concluded that maybe my experiment had been worth it. And as to #7 above: I did not have to print off a hard copy of my new essay for seminar on Sunday morning after all. I just brought my tablet to church and read it off the screen.

My doctor says that I am his most boring patient, because there is never anything wrong with me. I show up for my yearly appointment, my

Attentiveness—There It Is

blood pressure is good, my weight fluctuates within a five-pound range, my blood work is always fine—my only complaints are spring allergies, for which he says "take Claritin," and occasional sciatica problems, for which he suggests that I should stretch more. I have never been in a hospital overnight except when I was born, and I don't remember that. But Jeanne has had a number of things that have needed attention over the years, including back problems. One time as she suffered with excruciating back pain, a co-worker suggested that she get in touch with his father, Peter, who runs a chiropractic/acupuncture/Eastern medicine establishment within an hour's drive of Providence. Peter's business card says "Japanese Body Balance Shoppe and Acupuncture Clinic." Jeanne has always been far more adventurous when it comes to medical treatments than I am, so she immediately made an appointment and I went along for the ride.

Peter's treatment was so successful in just one session that he has become our "go-to" guy for just about everything. I even started getting "tune ups" with Peter after which, although I went in feeling fine, I came out feeling a lot better than fine. When I fell walking my dachshunds and jammed my shoulder badly a few summers ago, I am convinced that a session with Peter is what saved me from surgery. Jeanne and I revere Peter's almost-mystical abilities so much that after several years we talk about him as if he would have been a great healing partner for Jesus had he lived two thousand years ago.

Peter is a child of the sixties as Jeanne and I are; over time we have learned a lot of his life story, including how he as a Westerner became a trained practitioner of Eastern healing arts. He told us once of a horrible automobile accident he was in during his twenties that he barely survived, with dozens of broken bones and damaged internal organs. Skilled doctors and surgeons were able to fuse and stitch him back together, but he lived in excruciating pain until on a friend's advice and with nothing to lose he tried some "alternative" Eastern treatments. And the treatments worked—so well that subsequently he lived with his Japanese wife in Japan for several years training as an apprentice, then a master of *sotaiho*, a method of treatment I can only describe as a mixture of acupuncture, chiropracty, and aroma therapy. Peter describes his journey this way: "Western medicine saved my life, and Eastern medicine gave me my life back." Western medicine fixed Peter, in other words, and Eastern medicine healed him.

During a recent semester a central text in a course that a colleague and I were team teaching was Albert Camus's *The Plague*. A captivating story inviting many different levels of interpretation, *The Plague* raises important questions about living in the midst of danger, suffering, pain, and loss so destructive and pervasive that mere survival is at risk. Toward the end of the novel, one of the characters suggests a helpful way of sorting the complications out.

> All I maintain is that on this earth there are pestilences and there are victims, and it is up to us, so far as possible, not to join forces with the pestilences . . . . We should also grant a third category: that of the true healers. But it's a fact one doesn't come across many of them, and anyhow it must be a hard vocation. . . . I can at least try to discover how one attains to the third category; in other words, to peace.[14]

This passage frequently came up during the final oral exams with our thirty-eight students at the end of the semester as we asked each to identify persons we had studied during the semester who might count as "healers." In the midst of fascinating and insightful discussions, students often focused on a personal story that my teaching colleague Ray used during one of my lectures to illustrate the important concept of "attention" from Simone Weil (another author from the semester). Ray and his wife Pat are intimately involved with the Society of Saint Vincent de Paul, a Catholic relief society whose members strive to grow spiritually by offering person-to-person service to those in need. Pat and Ray frequently make home visits to such individuals and families in need. Ray described to the students that the typical home visit often consisted of making the client aware of the various services the society has that could address various needs and problems, including health care, food and clothing assistance, directing people to other agencies with needed services, and so on. With the best of intentions, such services were often offered without knowing in detail the history or story of the client and his or her family.

Then, as Ray described, after becoming aware of Simone Weil's concept of "attention," in which Weil says "The soul empties itself of all its own contents in order to receive into itself the being it is looking at, just as he is, in all his truth,"[15] he and Pat tried something different on their next home visit. Instead of immediately describing what they, as representatives of the society, could do for the person in need, Pat and Ray asked the client "What would you like to tell us? What is your story?" And for the next

14. Camus, *The Plague*, 253–54.
15. Weil, *Waiting*, 65.

hour, they listened to the woman tell her story without interruption. And this completely transformed the dynamic both of that conversation and of future home visits. Through listening without interruption and projection, Ray and Pat had established an atmosphere of healing rather than of one of fixing.

Attentiveness is the skill of seeing, of attending to the reality of something other than oneself without the filters of the self being in the way. It is a task of love that requires constant practice, as illustrated by Pat and Ray in their home visit. Pat and Ray had moved from considering the woman in front of them as a problem to be solved, or something broken in need of fixing, to a healing activity of seeing her, as Weil describes, "not as a unit in a collection, or a specimen from the social category labeled 'unfortunate,' but as a person, exactly like us, who was one day stamped with a special mark by affliction."[16] And this transforms everything. Being a healer begins with simply listening, for "The love of our neighbor in all its fullness simply means being able to say to him: 'What are you going through?'"[17] It begins not by asking "How can I solve your problem?" but rather by inviting the person in need to answer the question "Who are you?"

---

16. Ibid., 64.
17. Ibid.

5

Silence—Taking My Soul Wherever I Go

Not long ago I participated in an end-of-the-semester faculty seminar on Shakespeare's *King Lear*. The seminar, led by a Shakespeare scholar from the English department, was a welcome return to a text that I find both strikingly dark and strangely compelling every time I read it. I love Shakespeare and find his insights about human nature and the human condition more profound than any other author I've encountered, but I had not read this particular tragedy for a while. As always, the play blew me away, disturbed me, and left me wondering whether my colleagues might find some glimmers of hope and redemption in its lines that have always escaped me.

King Lear pushes to the limit a hypothesis that has a long and complicated pedigree: we live in a universe that is malign, at the very least indifferent, and human life within this universe is brutal, wretched, and meaningless. As various nasty and morally awful characters—including Lear's two older daughters—apparently prosper, those characters with even a shred of dignity, honor, or love—including his youngest daughter—are rejected and ultimately destroyed. By the end of the play, the stage is littered with the bodies of both the good and the bad, while a handful of dazed survivors are left to pick up the pieces. Naked in a driving storm in the middle of a heath, Lear rages that human beings are nothing but "poor, bare forked animals,"[1] living on a "great stage of fools."[2] Lear demands an answer to

1. Shakespeare, *King Lear*, III.iv.106.
2. Ibid., IV.vi.183.

the question "Is man no more than this?"[3] The blinded Gloucester despairingly directs his accusations heavenward: "As flies to wanton boys are we to th'gods; / They kill us for their sport."[4]

My colleagues and I ended two morning hours of seminar and another afternoon hour by viewing the final act of the play on screen with the 2008 movie version starring Ian MacKellan as Lear. It is a stark production with Beckett-like sparse staging. As character after character dies—Lear's three daughters, the evil Edmund, and ultimately Lear himself—and the stage is littered with corpses, the play ends with Edgar's final lines: "The weight of this sad time we must obey, / Speak what we feel, not what we ought to say."[5] Fade to black. The seminar leader asked us for our feelings, our impressions of what we had just seen, and for the first time in thirty years in academia I heard something I've never before heard when in the presence of twenty scholars: total silence. In obedience to Edgar's directive, no one felt obligated to say anything that "should" be said; at least for a minute or two, we were not professors ready to discuss the next topic to death, but human beings stunned into silence by Shakespeare's brilliant and disabling portrayal of a meaningless and hopeless world.

There are many times when silence is the only appropriate response. I learned this a number of years ago as I learned how silence sometimes is the key that opens doors long shut. Noon prayers at St. John's Abbey only take fifteen minutes, but at least eight to ten of those minutes are silent pauses between and amidst the three psalms assigned for the day. It took me a while to get the hang of the reading break at the end of each line that was about a second longer than I was expecting, as well to make it through the one-minute pause between each psalm without fidgeting or looking at my watch. After a couple of weeks, though, I found a space inside myself that the pace of noon prayer fit exactly. And I discovered for the first time what the psalmist means by "Be still, and know that I am God."[6] Silence has to do with stillness, with listening and quietness. Even in the cavernous Abbey, there are always sounds—the ventilation system, someone's cough, the rustle of papers. But something began to happen to me while sitting in the choir stalls. The quietness of disciplined monks, in the company of less disciplined non-monks, regularly helped me to notice, for the first time, an

3. Ibid., III.iv.102.
4. Ibid., IV.i.36-37.
5. Ibid., V.iii.329-30.
6. Ps 46:10.

internal space for God to inhabit and within which, amazingly enough, to perhaps say something.

On one particular day, the closing prayer had included the petition that God would assist us during the Lenten season in being responsive to "the fertility of silence." An evocative phrase, especially in a world in which the white noise of television, radio, the Internet, and just plain old daily life threatens to make silence into nothing more than a fossilized reminder of something that human beings used to have available. Some claim that "the devil is in the details"—I think that God is in the silence. I'm reminded of a couple of lines from a beautiful Advent song I heard a few years ago at a Lessons and Carols Service: "As we await you, O God of silence, we embrace your holy night." In response to our frequent complaints that God never says anything, perhaps we need to embrace the fertility of divine silence.

It takes practice and diligence to allow silence to be fertile, as I was reminded at the end of our *King Lear* seminar. After what seemed like a very long silence, someone made a comment, then someone else followed up, and pretty soon we were doing what academics do in every context and setting—talking. Several people referenced the silence that preceded the talking and began to analyze what it was about both the play and the film adaptation that caused us to be temporarily wordless. But with Edgar's final lines in mind, our first reaction was most in line with "Speak what we feel"—except that our feelings were, at least for a few moments, deeper than words could express.

I came out of my months with the monks embracing a mantra from Psalm 131: "Truly I have set my soul in silence and in peace; As a weaned child on its mother's breast, so is my soul."[7] Silence reminds me, as a first grader once told Kathleen Norris, "to take my soul with me wherever I go."[8] When I remember that God is in the space of silence and peace within, I realize that the divine's response to my need is something entirely unexpected but absolutely Godlike. In an encounter with divine reality we do not hear a voice but acquire a voice; and the voice we acquire is our own.

Late in a recent fall semester I did all of the things a college professor needs to do when attending an out-of-town conference while classes are in session. I put up an "away" message on Outlook announcing my absence for four days from the administrative saddle because of traveling to a

---

7. Ps 131:2.
8. Norris, *Amazing Grace*, 17.

conference, let my "inner circle" blog circulation list know that they would have to do something other than wait expectantly for my usual 7:30 AM Friday blog post on a particular upcoming Friday, arranged for my teaching teammates to cover the Friday afternoon seminar on the *Aeneid* that I would be missing, and generally covered my academic ass. No biggie—everyone knows that giving papers at a conference is part of the academic life that requires rearranging classes and office hours on occasion.

But I was not giving a paper. I wasn't even going to a conference. I was going to a *retreat*, which in most corners of academia is tantamount to going to a sixties love-in. The name of the retreat, located at the Episcopal House of Prayer on the campus that is home to my beloved Saint John's Abbey, was "Prayer in the Cave of the Heart," led by a Benedictine monk who is the prior of a hermitage in Big Sur where I spent a week several summers ago. It's a good thing that I have not needed tenure or promotion points for some time now, because participation in such an event would have carried negative academic weight. The value of going to such a retreat in the middle of the semester in the eyes of the Committee on Academic Rank and Tenure on our campus would be similar to what the psalmist says about the ungodly: "In the balances they go up; they are together lighter than a breath."[9] The fact that I perceived several months ago that this retreat at this point in the semester would be good for my soul would be irrelevant to the committee—"But will this produce a peer-reviewed article? Probably not? No tenure or promotion for you!" But I've been around long enough to have been on that committee myself for a couple of years, convincing myself every Friday afternoon that I was qualified to mess with other people's lives. If I determine that a trip to the middle-of-nowhere Minnesota is what is needed to keep my spirit, soul, and body centered and willing to inhabit the same mortal container, that committee can't do anything about it.

Human beings are funny creatures; human beings on retreat are even funnier. The average age of the twenty-four people gathered at this one was probably a bit over my fifty-nine years, with women outnumbering men two to one. The women all looked alike—tall, thin, wearing glasses, with roughly the same short haircut (with the exception of one woman with a long braid who looked like a refugee from the sixties and who was the only person of either gender attending with hair longer than mine). It turned out that four or five of these women were ordained Episcopal clergy from the Diocese of North Dakota. The guys were a bit more varied in appearance,

9. Ps 62:9.

beardless and bearded, bald and haired, thin and not so thin, including one heavyset guy who fell asleep during meditation in the oratory and snored really loudly. Twice. Everyone on retreat walks the same way, with a slow and intentionally reverent gait similar to how zombies walk when they are staggering toward you in the movies. Everyone and everything slows down at a retreat, at least at the ones I go to, which is a good thing.

Just as the other two times I have attended retreats at the House of Prayer, silence was observed from the conclusion of evening prayer around nine until the end of lunch the next day; the only exceptions were during teaching sessions with whomever was running the retreat. In these sessions we were allowed to ask questions, but only if they were good ones. I love silence. Silence is good. But not when packed into a small dining room seated six to a circular table for breakfast and lunch during what is quaintly called "the Great Silence." The sounds of people chewing their food while uncomfortably looking anywhere but at each other may be an important part of some people's spiritual practice, but it doesn't do anything for me. There is no one more introverted than I am, but even I breathed a sigh of relief when lunch ended and we all were allowed to speak for the next nine hours or so.

Other than the leader of the retreat, who came from California, I was the person who had traveled the farthest. My flights were such that I was the first arrival early on Thursday afternoon, a few hours before the retreat officially began at dinner. After touching base with the director of the retreat house who is a friend (largely because between us Jeanne and I have been to five retreats at this place over the past five years) and moving my stuff into my room, I went into the beautiful large living room area with a glass wall overlooking the adjacent forest, made a cup of tea, and sat down to read Anne Lamott's latest book. *Tea?* Since when did I start drinking tea? I have been a dedicated coffee drinker (more like a coffee swiller) since my teenage years. Jeanne was a tea drinker when we met years ago and still drinks tea on occasion as well as coffee, but it's not me. Tea is for pussies. Who can spare the precious seconds wasted with opening the tea bag envelope, waiting for the tea to steep in hot water for an interminable minute or so, then figuring out how to drink it with a tea bag floating in it? By the time all that happens I will have swilled a paper cup of coffee, black since I can't spare the time to add cream and sugar, and be back to the important business of whatever I'm doing—since everything I do is obviously important business. I don't drink tea.

Except on retreat. As noted earlier, human beings on retreat are funny creatures—I am no exception. Making myself tea instead of coffee for my first of many hot drinks over the four-day retreat was not a conscious decision—I didn't even notice I had done it until I sat down to read. But my body knew something my mind didn't know. Transitioning from an eighty to one-hundred-hour work week to a four-day retreat is not as easy as flipping a switch. Slowing down, mindfulness, deliberation, and attentiveness—all those good things that I've begun to incorporate into my days but that slip through my fingers easily when swamped by real life—need practice. And taking the time to make a cup of tea (which I actually really like the taste of) rather than throwing another several ounces of coffee down my pie hole was a good place to start. The retreat director encouraged us to take the time to pay attention to what you are doing, do each thing as it comes, and wait to see what comes next. I know this. Sometimes I even do it. But this retreat was an opportunity to drop fully into the space that I'd been skimming over or dodging around for weeks. And to notice that this space is always there waiting—my deepest (and best) me.

"This thing better have good news in it," I said as I unwrapped my P. F. Chang's fortune cookie. And it did.

You will receive your heart's desire.

Great, I thought. *I wonder what the hell* that *is.*

It had not been a good day. That morning I had received a rejection email from the ##### Foundation, to whom I had applied for sabbatical funding the previous fall. In typical rejection letter style, I was informed that "We received seventy-six applications and awarded ten grants. The quality of the grant proposals made the work of the selection committee challenging indeed. I regret to inform you . . . blah, blah, blah." This sucked big time because of the two funding proposals I sent out last fall, this was the one I thought I had the much better shot at. The other proposal involved a semester residency at a think tank on the campus of a prestigious university that shall remain nameless but whose name rhymes with "voter game." The email I received from the think tank confirming receipt of my full proposal application contained the following throwaway line at the end: "Please note that our fellowships are very competitive, with past annual acceptance rates of 4 to 9 percent." Nice.

I do not handle rejection well—not that I've had a lot of it in my career. I have never been an adjunct professor. Both teaching positions I have held were tenure track. Each time I got an on-campus interview I won the job. My ascent of the tenure and promotion ladder had only one easily correctable glitch. I have spent twenty-two years teaching at the same college, loving every minute of those years (or at least 95 percent of them). Three books, a number of articles, a teaching award, two significant administrative posts—I'm not writing this to impress anyone, but rather to illustrate my inner dialogue every time I *do* get rejected. I immediately start trying to convince myself that I'm really okay, despite the fact that the ##### Foundation did not deem my sabbatical project worth spending a dime on.

These are the times when I am grateful both for my training in classical music and for being forced to memorize lots of verses from the Bible in my growing up years. As soon as I read the cookie's promise that I will receive my heart's desire, my memory tapes started playing a song I hadn't thought of in years, perhaps decades. It is a solo from Felix Mendelssohn's oratorio *Elijah*, with the seemingly appropriate (but very difficult to actually do) title "O Rest in the Lord." I hate it when this happens, because the last thing I felt like doing that day was waiting or resting. My heart's desire is to have funding for my freaking sabbatical project, and what I considered to be my most likely source of that funding just said "thanks for playing, but no." So "rest in the Lord, wait patiently for him, and he shall give thee thy heart's desires?" Whatever—I don't think so.

Mendelssohn's *Elijah* is a dramatic musical treatment of various episodes from Elijah's life as described in the Jewish Scriptures, including his getting to ride in a flaming chariot to heaven once his prophesying work was over. In part one of the oratorio Elijah has one of the greatest and most spectacular successes any prophet ever has experienced or will experience. In a high stakes contest with the prophets of Baal on top of Mount Carmel, God has shown up in impressive fashion, as Elijah calls down fire that consumes the sacrifice, the wood on the altar, the stones that the altar is made out of, and the water surrounding it. The people fall on their faces and cry "The Lord, He is God! The Lord, He is God!" In the exhilarating glow of spectacular success, Elijah has the 500 prophets of Baal taken down the mountain to a brook and executed.

But then King Ahab reports to his wife, Queen Jezebel—a woman who in terms of evil and just plain nastiness puts Lady Macbeth to shame—what has happened to her prophets, and everything changes. By the beginning of part two, Elijah is fleeing for his life into the wilderness. As the First Kings story tells us, the exhausted prophet eventually collapses into a fetal position under a broom tree and has a classic drama queen moment: "It is enough; now, O Lord, take away my life, for I am no better than my ancestors."[10] And for once, God does something practical. While Elijah sleeps, an angel makes him breakfast; when Elijah stirs, the angel serves him the meal, then provides entertainment by singing a lovely setting of Psalm 37—which 3,000 years or so later makes it into Mendelssohn's *Elijah* as "O Rest in the Lord."

Mendelssohn's text rearranges a few of the verses from Psalm 37, but captures the point perfectly. For those who are fretting and stressed about what the future holds, the psalmist provides a set of simple promises.

> Take delight in the Lord, and he will give you the desires of your heart.
> Commit your way to the Lord; trust in him, and he will act.
> Be still before the Lord, and wait patiently for him;
> Do not fret over those who prosper in their way,
> Over those who carry out evil devices.[11]

Although this text is steeped in a religious perspective that I became familiar with before I learned to walk, the psalmist's advice sounds remarkably like what the ancient Stoics tell us—be clear about what is in your control and what is not. Don't waste energy trying to control the latter; instead, create your moral and spiritual home out of the former. What I *can* control is how I process and respond to what the largely uncontrollable world hands me—disappointment, dashed hopes, unexpected opportunities, and a hell of a lot of the mundane, daily grind. The verbs in Psalm 37 are telling: trust, commit, be still, be patient, don't worry, and take delight. These are the core of a life of centeredness and peace—something available even when things don't go my way.

As I venture into the last third of my years on earth, I realize that I have often received my heart's desire, and it almost never has been what I would have predicted. I'm not sure I even know what my heart's desire *is* going forward, but I do want to tune my inner receptors more and more carefully so that I will recognize it when it crosses my radar screen. Jeanne occasionally points out that the word *silent* is made of the same letters as the word *listen*. Worth remembering.

---

10. 1 Kgs 19:4.
11. Ps 37:4–5, 7.

One recent Sunday, the text from the Jewish scriptures was a familiar passage from Isaiah:

> The wolf shall live with the lamb, the leopard shall lie down with the kid; the calf and the lion and the fatling together, and a little child shall lead them. The cow and the bear shall graze, their young shall lie down together; and the lion shall eat straw like the ox. The nursing child shall play over the hole of the asp, and the weaned child shall put its hand on the adder's den.[12]

The eighteenth-century Quaker artist Edward Hicks painted many interpretations of this text, a series called "The Peaceable Kingdom." The rector had a print of one of these propped up at the altar for our viewing pleasure as we approached for communion. Hicks's artistic rendition of Isaiah's vision is complete with rather flat representations of all the above animals plus three children, all hanging out on a grassy knoll with pop-eyed and glazed looks that have all the earmarks of drug inducement. The promise of the day's readings was a future world of peace where natural enemies will no longer be enemies. In the religious tradition of my youth, we considered Isaiah's peaceable kingdom either to be a description of heaven itself, or of God's millennial kingdom of 1,000 years that would occur after the second coming of Christ and the tribulation in which, after a lot of violence and judgment, the bad guys would be destroyed and only we good guys would remain. When we prayed "Thy kingdom come, thy will be done," we really meant "Please come back soon and rescue us from this totally crappy and ruined world."

This same passage from Isaiah was one of the readings a few years ago for a service focused on an international day of prayer for peace. Another of that morning's readings was also from Isaiah, who in chapter two invites us to go to "the mountain of the Lord" where, at some unspecified future time, the Lord will reign supreme and human beings will be acting quite differently than we do now.

> They will beat their swords into ploughshares, and their spears into sickles; nation shall not lift up sword against nation, neither shall they learn war any more.[13]

Whatever Isaiah was seeing in this memorable vision, it sure isn't the present. Although the writer of Ecclesiastes says there is "a time for war, and

12. Isa 11:6–8.
13. Isa 2:4.

a time for peace,"[14] the time for war has stretched for as long as human existence, and its end doesn't appear imminent. So what am I supposed to be praying for on the day of prayer for peace and every other day? What can I do to help bring about world peace? Put "Visualize Whirled Peas" and "Who Would Jesus Bomb?" bumper stickers on my car? Commit random acts of kindness? Sing "Give Peace a Chance" along with John and Yoko? Why not just spit into the wind and be done with it?

One possible place to begin is to remember that the kingdom of God for which we pray, the peaceable kingdom, is here. "The kingdom of God is among you."[15] The peaceable kingdom begins in me, just as every one of Isaiah's beasts is in me. I am a wolf, a lamb, a leopard, a goat, a calf, a lion, a cow, a bear, an ox, an adder, and an asp, as well as some other things Isaiah didn't mention. There is probably a dachshund and a Boston terrier in there too. And, lest I forget, both a nursing child and a weaned child. The key to establishing a peaceable kingdom within me is not to tame the scary beasts and put the fuzzy and cuddly ones in charge. Rather, it's welcoming them all, allowing each its place, and not getting nervous when the lion and lamb decide to sit next to each other. As I welcome and release each of the beasts, I commit myself, at least for today, to following the example of the psalmist in Psalm 131:

> Truly I have set my soul in silence and peace. As a weaned child on its mother's breast, so is my soul.[16]

---

14. Eccl 3:8.
15. Luke 17:21.
16. Ps 131:2.

6

Grace—Having the Right *Niyyah*

I wonder what my life would look like if I really believed this. How would my life be different if I was not scared, if I really believed that I am fully and totally loved by God?[1] —Nadia Bolz-Weber

A decade ago, I attended a writers' conference for the first time in my life. My workshop was "Literary Essay"; each of the fifteen members wrote daily 500-word essays, which were submitted to colleagues for critique and (hopefully) helpful evaluation. My essays tended to praise the virtues of my dachshund and the Boston Red Sox, while frequently delving into my struggles with faith, God, religion, and my own very human inadequacies. About halfway through the two-week conference, during a critique session when I was on the hot seat with my most recent submission, one of my colleagues said "You write so negatively about yourself in your essays. You seem like a really nice guy—why do you have such a negative self-image?" Other colleagues murmured their agreement.

My immediate reaction was not defensive—despite being very confident in some aspects of my life, my self-image over the years has been more negative than positive. My internal reaction instead was a quick realization that I might be the only person in the room who didn't think he or she was

1. Bolz-Weber, *Accidental*, 70.

pretty much okay. My fourteen colleagues were a diverse bunch, including a specialist in Chinese history, an archaeologist, a high school student, a vice president of an international banking firm, a local politician, a poet who just published her first collection of poems, several self-described "writers' conference rats" (one was at this conference for the seventh straight year), and our workshop leader, a nationally known essayist and columnist who had just published his third novel. And they were mildly uncomfortable with my explicit self-doubts and honesty about my shortcomings and failures.

I was in the midst of some difficult internal stuff that summer, but I'll bet many of my colleagues were too. I realize now that what really made me different from them is original sin—it has defined me for as long as I can remember, and they knew nothing of it. I learned early on that I don't measure up, that I'm not good enough, that "nothing good dwells within me."[2] And it's not an exclusively Christian idea; the psalmist says "I was born guilty, a sinner when my mother conceived me."[3] We're all screwed from the start. Some make a bigger deal of this than others. Martin Luther likened divine grace to a layer of freshly fallen snow covering a pile of shit. And guess who the pile is. Grace doesn't transform the pile—shit is still shit—but it covers it so that its smell is not quite as offensive and it doesn't look quite as disgusting.

This is a wonderful foundation upon which to build a positive self-image, but it's the engine that drives a lot of religious activity. I remember that many years ago the Catholic Dominican priest Matthew Fox was excommunicated for teaching, among other things, that the doctrine of original sin is wrong and for writing books with titles like *Original Blessing*. He became an Episcopal priest after his excommunication, which makes sense—we Episcopalians will take anyone as long as they appreciate good liturgy and have sufficiently liberal social and political commitments. And to be honest, after twenty-five years as a recovering Protestant involved in Catholic higher education, I've discovered that most Catholics I know take original sin far less seriously than the people I grew up with. Catholics pay lip service to the notion that human beings need divine help; my people meant it. They told me I deserved to go to hell and would undoubtedly end up there unless I was "right with Jesus." And my workshop colleagues wondered why I wrote negatively about myself.

2. Rom 7:18.
3. Ps 51:5.

Many groups of people, both religious and otherwise, speak as if they have a corner on guilt and inadequacy. I knew no Catholics when I was growing up, but now that I spend a large portion of my time with them professionally and have many Catholic friends, I know all about Catholic guilt, despite the fact that they don't talk about original sin much. I was surprised to find out that Catholics think that Catholic guilt is uniquely debilitating, just as they were surprised to find out that I know all about it; I just call it Baptist guilt. I've even participated in good-natured debates about whose guilt is more paralyzing. Everyone knows about Jewish guilt, Irish guilt, and so on. We apparently don't need religious doctrine to tell us that we are inadequate and flawed. We just need to be human beings. John Henry Newman wrote that just observing what's going on around us with the slightest care reveals that "the human race is implicated in some terrible aboriginal calamity."[4] That's a wonderfully British, urbane, nineteenth-century way of saying "we're really f–ked up." There's something fundamentally wrong at our core, and we all know it. Many manage to cope with this by ignoring it, by refusing to include it in their vocabulary, by defining themselves in terms according to which they can be acceptable and successful. "I'm okay, you're okay"—but as Emily Dickinson suggests in "The World is not Conclusion," there's still a "tooth that nibbles at the soul"[5]—we're *not* okay.

A few years ago, toward the end of a lovely lunch conversation, a new friend and colleague observed that "it's hard being a person," in the same factual tone of voice in which he might have said "this coffee is cold." I said in response that I knew, years earlier, that Simone Weil is my kind of woman when I read in her notebooks that in her estimation, "human life is impossible."[6] So often, that's where I begin. I'm not okay and I need help. And the first step forward has to be one of trust, of a hope that this can be better. Anne Lamott defines grace as when "suddenly you're in a different universe from the one where you were stuck, and there was absolutely no way for you get there on your own."[7] But how does one tap into the transcendent energy of unexpected gratuitous moments in order to energize all the days, weeks, and months until the next such moment? To experience grace is one thing, but to integrate it into your life is quite another. How does one build a daily life around occasional grace?

4. Newman, *Apologia*, 163.
5. Dickinson, *Complete Poems*, 501.
6. Weil, *Gravity*, 86.
7. Lamott, *Small Victories*, 149.

GRACE—HAVING THE RIGHT NIYYAH

As Jeanne and I waited at one of our fine local theaters for Henrik Ibsen's *Hedda Gabler* to begin, I read an interesting anecdote in the program. Thornton Wilder once told Tennessee Williams that he thought Blanche DuBois was too complex a character for the theater. To which Williams replied, "People are complex, Thorn." A century earlier, Henrik Ibsen built that truth about human beings into his characters and plays. My knowledge of Ibsen and his work has been gathered over the years from teaching in a team-taught course where my literature colleague has occasionally chosen one of Ibsen's controversial and fascinating plays for the students to grapple with, ranging from *An Enemy of the People* to *The Wild Duck* and *A Doll's House*. Ibsen's penchant for ripping the veil off late-nineteenth-century bourgeois Norwegian society, pushing his readers' and audience's faces up against topics that decent people would just as soon not consider, and especially his willingness to populate his plays with female characters who explode the stereotypes of dutiful wife and devoted mother, caused his plays to not only be banned in several countries during his lifetime (he was nicknamed "Ibscene") but also make them sound to a twenty-first-century audience as if they were written yesterday.

Ibsen prefers shadow to light and seldom goes far before revealing something dark and sinister lying beneath the surface of even the most pleasant persons and ordinary circumstances. Hedda Gabler, a newlywed just returned from her honeymoon with her husband George, a newly minted PhD (philosophy, no less!) who is expecting a plum appointment at the local university, finds herself situated in a large new house ready to be furnished with whatever furniture she fancies. George is clearly infatuated with his beautiful new wife, whom everyone describes (to her increasing annoyance) as "glowing." But appearances are deceiving; only a few minutes into the play we find that Hedda is complicated to the core. Another short essay in the program guide reports that Hedda has been described by critics as "sinister, degenerate, repellent, lunatic, a monster in the shape of a woman, with a soul too small even for human sin." A bit over the top, perhaps, but she actually is just about all of that. But she is also charismatic, has a razor sharp wit, crackles with energy, and as if by magic causes everyone in the room to dance to her tune.

As I watched the play unfold on the stage fifteen feet away, I realized that Hedda is not necessarily a bad person bent on the destruction of everything she touches. In this performance she was brilliantly played with the energy of a trapped animal, like a tiger or lion in a zoo cage pacing back and forth restlessly, looking everywhere for a way to escape, and devouring everything and everyone unfortunate enough to fall within her reach. She finds herself in a world in which the only acceptable roles for a woman are roles that she not only would reject if given the opportunity but for which she is also completely unsuited. In a twisted version of Socrates's observation that some lives are not worth living, Hedda strikes out more and more desperately as she feels the walls closing in. When there is no more room to move or breathe, she chooses to die rather than to live under these circumstances.

Sixteen freshmen and I encountered another trapped human being the day after Jeanne and I saw *Hedda Gabler*. That day's seminar was the culmination of New Testament week, in which the students had already read the Gospel of Mark for a setup lecture; the assignment for seminar was Luke, Acts, and Romans. We spent the bulk of the two hours considering various passages in both Luke and Acts where the very clear requirements of following Jesus set the behavior bar so high that clearly no normal human being could reach it. Iris Murdoch once commented that it would have made sense if in the Sermon on the Mount Jesus had said something like "Be ye therefore slightly improved,"[8] but he didn't. Instead he said "Be perfect, therefore, as your heavenly Father is perfect."[9] Even at eighteen or nineteen years old, my students had enough life experience to know that the gospel standard is one that is impossible for flawed creatures such as we are to meet.

No one has ever described the human predicament more effectively than Paul at the end of Romans 7—I took the students there toward the end of seminar.

> I do not understand my own actions. For I do not do what I want, but I do the very thing I hate . . . . For I know that nothing good dwells within me . . . I can will what is right, but I cannot do it. For I do not do the good I want, but the evil I do not want is what I do . . . . Wretched man that I am! Who will rescue me from this body of death?[10]

Hedda found herself trapped in circumstances in which she could not flourish, grow, survive, or even breathe. Paul finds himself in the same situation,

---

8. Murdoch, *Existentialists*, 350.
9. Matt 5:48.
10. Rom 7:15, 18–19, 24.

Grace—Having the Right Niyyah

but with much greater scope, knowing what must or should be done and finding himself completely incapable of doing it. Bottom line, this is the human condition. No wonder we often strike out in frustration and anger at whatever is within reach. However we came to be in this predicament, we cannot work or will our way out of it.

Then in a masterful reversal of just a few lines, Paul provides a way out so compelling that it is hardly to be believed, a way packed with hope and promise.

> There is therefore now no condemnation for those who are in Christ Jesus. For the law of the Spirit of life in Christ Jesus has set you free from the law of sin and of death. For God has done what the law . . . could not do by sending his own Son . . . .[11]

It is this hope and promise that both uniquely defines the Christian faith and can keep a flawed, seriously damaged creature from descending into Paul's despair or Hedda's destructive rage. For every frustrated "I can't do this!" there is an "Of course you can't. But help is available."

I recently listened to a Krista Tippett interview on NPR with Rami Nashashibi, a professor of sociology who is also the founder and executive director of the Inner-City Muslim Action Network in Chicago. Particularly memorable was a brief exchange toward the end of the interview, when Nashashibi told the story of how his four-year-old daughter came to understand the meaning of her name. He explained that his daughter's name, "Niyyah," is in both Swahili and Arabic the word for "spiritual intention." Muslims are asked before they pray or perform any act of service, before they engage in anything that has a sense of worship associated with it, whether it is being done for the right *niyyah*. Is it being done for the right purpose? Are you attempting to get fame or credit? As Nashashibi tells it,

> there was a song that had used her name in that way and the light went off in the middle of it and she turned over to me on the couch and asked me "Daddy, do you have the right *niyyah*?" Honestly, I looked at her and I didn't have an answer for I think a good twenty seconds. She nodded her head and said, "No, probably not."[12]

This four-year-old's simple question has stuck with me ever since. So has her response to her father's lack of response. It's hard enough to figure out

---

11. Rom 8:1–3.
12. Tippett and Nashashibi, "A New Coming Together," lines 445–50.

what the right thing to do is on a daily basis; adding that it should be done with the right intention, for the right reasons, seems like piling on.

Over the years I have frequently asked my students in various classes "What is more important—*what* you do, or *why* you do it? Actions or intentions?" They usually split roughly down the middle. And so do the great moral philosophers. There is one tradition that says only results matter (since they can be observed and measured publically) and intentions are irrelevant. Then there is another tradition claiming that results are irrelevant—the true measure of the moral life is internal. Were your intentions pure? Was your heart in the right place? If so, then you are morally in the clear, even if the results of your intended action go "tits up" (to quote my brother-in-law).

It doesn't take my students very long to realize that the "results or intentions" question is a false dichotomy. Because in truth, we care about both. Four-year-old Niyyah is right—we not only want the right thing to be done, but for it to be done with the right *niyyah*, the right intention or reason. And that sucks, because it takes things straight into the human heart. For those who profess the Christian faith, it also takes things straight into the world of grace.

The first thing I ever learned from Scripture about the human heart as a young boy was from Jeremiah: "The heart is devious above all else; it is perverse—who can understand it?"[13] Far less attention was paid to the Psalm that is recited in liturgical churches during the Ash Wednesday liturgy: "Create in me a clean heart, O God, and put a new and right spirit within me. . . . Restore to me the joy of your salvation, and sustain in me a willing spirit."[14] Straight from the Jewish scriptures is both the problem of and the solution for right intentions. As a flawed human being, I am incapable of consistently doing things for the right reason. But through divine grace the heart is changed and turned toward the good. We seldom have the right *niyyah*, if that depends on our own energies and strength. But when the divine gets involved, everything changes.

The mystery of grace is exactly that—a mystery. Strangely enough, divine grace enters the world through flawed human beings. Grace is something to be channeled, to be lived, not systematized and turned into dogma or doctrine. Through many years of cancer treatments, poet and essayist Christian Wiman learned to hear God, then to channel God, in the

---

13. Jer 17:9.
14. Ps 51:10, 12.

most unlikely places, the very places where divine grace apparently resides. Wiman writes that

> God speaks to us by speaking through us, and any meaning we arrive at in this life is composed of the irreducible details of the life that is around us at any moment.... All too often the task to which we are called is simply to show a kindness to the irritating person in the cubicle next to us, or to touch the face of a spouse from whom we ourselves have been long absent, letting grace wake love from our intense, self-enclosed sleep.[15]

The right *niyyah* is not the result of struggle, training, or calculation. All I have to do to have the right *niyyah* is to open my heart and let it out.

> What I crave now is that integration, some speech that is true to the transcendent nature of grace yet adequate to the hard reality in which daily faith operates.[16]

In my early years of teaching, I used to include one of Woody Allen's insights in the syllabus for every one of my classes: "80 percent of success is showing up." I don't use Woody's quote any more, since it doesn't mention that if 80 percent of success is showing up, the other 20 percent is being prepared when you show up. "Be prepared and show up" is also the key to divine encounters.

Be prepared. In Psalm 42 the psalmist writes "As a deer longs for flowing streams, so my soul longs for you, O God. My soul thirsts for God, for the living God. When shall I come and behold the face of God?"[17] Preparation is energized by desire, not the mind. I've occasionally described myself to my colleagues or students as a "God-obsessed" person. Fatemeh Keshavarz puts the question beautifully: "How is one to nurture this God buried like a ruin in the treasure of one's being and let it permeate all of life?"[18] Most important to answering that question is the word that begins the Rule of St. Benedict: "Listen." Shut up and be quiet. If preparation were primarily about what you know and what you've read, I'd be in decent shape. Only when my sabbatical experiences several years ago included a daily commitment to quietness did I begin to realize that, for me at least, preparation for God requires me to stop thinking and start listening.

---

15. Wiman, *Bright Abyss*, 94.
16. Ibid., 4.
17. Ps 42:1–3.
18. Tippett and Keshavarz, "The Ecstatic Faith," lines 414–15.

Show up. This is more about internal awareness than external place. When I'm too busy, too stressed, or too lazy to see anything other than whatever is an inch in front of my nose, I'm failing to show up. When I assume that I know that these texts, those places, these people, and those situations can't possibly be vehicles for contact with the divine, I'm failing to show up. When I continue to forage through the books and experiences where I've bumped into the transcendent in the past, presuming that God will remain there on my terms, I'm becoming an idolater rather than showing up. When I rely heavily on my brain, with which I'm most familiar, rather than my heart, which I'm not as comfortable with, I'm failing to show up.

We live in a reality soaked in transcendence, sacramental to its core. Everything is important—nothing is disposable. Once at a workshop the leader frequently said that two things are key to the spiritual life—"Be where you are," and "Do what you're doing." Sounds easy, but just try it—it's a never-ending challenge to be present every moment of the day. But I don't want to miss anything. Although I'm a very slow study, Annie Dillard's simple observation is beginning to seep in. "Beauty and grace are performed whether or not we will or sense them. The least we can do is be there."[19]

When my sons were young, one of the most important distinctions in their estimation, when food was the issue, was "is it fast or slow food?" In other words, how much of my important schedule is this eating event going to take up? Fast food—McDonald's, Wendy's, or Burger King if going out; fish sticks, hot dogs, sandwiches if staying in—was obviously preferred. Slow food—any place where you have to sit down and wait if going out; anything involving more than five minutes of preparation time and that you would not be consuming in front of the television if eating in—was acceptable only if given sufficient warning. Going out to a slow food restaurant required preparation, including which coloring books to bring, psychological calming techniques, a consideration of the expected guest list, and so on. People would often comment about how well these two little kids managed to keep themselves occupied without fidgeting or complaint for a much longer period of time than any child should be required to wait for food. That's only because they knew how to prepare.

In *Thinking, Fast and Slow*, Daniel Kahneman distinguishes between two types of thinking that all of us come equipped with. Fast thinking, on

---

19. Dillard, *Pilgrim*, 10.

the one hand, is the intuitive, almost unconscious way that we tend to make quick, snap judgments about events, people, choices, and even our life paths. Relying on emotion, memory, and hard-wired rules of thumb, much of our daily existence runs on fast-thinking autopilot. On the other hand, slow thinking is much more deliberate, conscious, attentive, self-aware, and—well—slower. According to Kahneman, the human mind is a hilariously muddled compromise between these incompatible modes of thought.

Most of us rely on fast thinking the majority of the time, even though we know that such thinking is often inaccurate and shot through with bias and prejudice. Why do we? At least on the surface, the answer clearly is "It's easier." Slow thinking laboriously checks the facts against the appearances, critically evaluates information, but can be lazy and easily distracted. Our slow thinking self is more than happy to turn things over to fast thinking simply because it conserves time and effort. Why take the time to consider the relevant details and nuances of a political candidate's positions when it is so much quicker and easier to label her as a "conservative," a "liberal," a "socialist," or a "Tea Partier" and move on? Why expend the effort to actually get to know a new colleague or neighbor when it is much simpler to label him as "one of them" and go to lunch?

When the stakes are high, when one's spiritual health and growth are at stake, the fast and slow distinction becomes far more than an interesting topic of conversation. Is the Christian life more like fast or slow food? Is it more like McDonald's or the Four Seasons? The Christian narrative is full of fast food events—Pentecost, Christmas, Easter—instant gratification events at the heart of belief that are so filling and satisfying that one could imagine that this is the exclusive food that fuels the life of faith. Each of us has had our own fast food experiences, times when the veil between the mundane human and glorious divine is pierced, even for a moment, in some unforgettable way. What more does one need?

Plenty. Was Pentecost, for instance, enough to sustain those who experienced it when, weeks or months later, they were alone in chains waiting for torture or execution? Will your most spectacular, transcendent moment from the past be enough to get you through the stress of parenting, the tragedy of loss, a divorce, being fired from your job, an illness, or simply the daily grind? If slow food is analogous to delayed gratification, then much—perhaps most—of the life of faith is slow food. Waiting, attending, struggling, just being, all the time wondering if you are ever going to get food again. That conversion experience, that healing, that moment that you vibrated with the presence of God, are all distant memories. And one cannot eat memories.

Fast thinking might convince us that an occasional trip to the McDonald's of faith is good enough. A few milestones, both doctrinal and personal, become the sole sustenance of faith, bolstered by some quick and easy rules of thumb and prescribed ways of behaving. Go to church, say your prayers, maybe read your Bible on occasion. Our slow-thinking selves eventually are willing to concede that this has to be enough, because what else is there? The answer lies in some of the food analogies that Jesus uses in the Gospels. "I am the bread of life," he said. "Whoever comes to me will never be hungry."[20] "Those who drink of the water that I will give them will never be thirsty,"[21] he tells the Samaritan woman at the well. The source of life, the food we need, is not in the fast food of events, of churches, nor is it in the slow food of waiting interminably for something to happen. It is in the regular, daily supply of nourishment that is in us "a spring of water gushing up to eternal life."[22]

During my one visit to Paris for a conference, I skipped papers and walked the city as much as time would allow. I saw firsthand that Parisians really *do* walk down the street holding a cell phone to one ear while carrying a baguette under their arm. Tearing off and eating a piece while walking down the sidewalk is as habitual to them as breathing. Maybe that's how the life of faith should be. We don't have to go shopping for the bread of life at either a fast or slow food establishment. It's with us all the time.

---

20. John 6:35.
21. John 4:14.
22. John 4:14.

7

Faith—Dealing with the "F" Word

A conversation amongst a bunch of guys at a sports bar waiting for the big game to begin:

"Dude, I've got one for you. There are these seven brothers named Aaron, Bill, Carl, Dave, Eric, Fred, and George. Aaron's the oldest one and he marries his high school girlfriend Paula. But he dies and Bill marries Paula because he thinks it's the right thing to do."

"That's kind of weird. Is Paula hot?"

"What does that matter?"

"If I was Bill, I wouldn't marry my sister-in-law unless she was hot."

"Never mind that—it's irrelevant. So after a couple of years Bill gets hit by a bus on the way to work and Carl, the next brother, marries Paula. But he dies too and so Dave marries Paula."

"How do they know that Paula isn't some kind of lunatic who marries guys then kills them? I saw a movie like that once."

"Dude, it's not like that. Dave and Paula are married for a while then Dave gets cancer and dies, so Eric marries Paula."

"This is so f--ked up! So then Eric dies and she marries Fred, then Fred dies and she marries George?"

"Yup. Then George and Paula are flying to Cancun for their honeymoon, the plane crashes, and they both die."

"Why the hell are you telling us this stupid story? Who cares?"

"The question is, in heaven, who is Paula going to be married to: Aaron, Bill, Carl, Dave, Eric, Fred, or George?"

"Are there any kids involved?"

"No—none of the guys lived long enough for there to be any kids."

"She'll be married to the last one—they were still married when she died."

"She'll be married to the first one—that's the only one that really counts."

"She'll be married to the one she loved the most."

"She'll be married to the one she had the best sex with."

"I heard that female praying mantises eat the head of their partner while having sex. Paula kinda sounds like that."

"Shut the hell up, guys—the game's starting!"

Put a few beers into a bunch of guys, and this is the sort of conversation that emerges. Except this conversation isn't from a sports bar. It is from Luke's gospel,[1] and the conversation is between a bunch of Sadducees and Jesus.

Among other things, the Sadducees did not believe in the resurrection of the dead. So why are they proposing this preposterous one wife for seven brothers scenario to Jesus? Not because they really want to know what he thinks will happen in heaven—they don't even believe that heaven exists. No, they are trying to expose this guy from Nazareth as the bumpkin from the sticks that they think he is. They have heard rumors that he believes in the resurrection of the dead, so they immediately go to the most ridiculous scenario they can come up with, just to make him look like a fool. Jesus shows remarkable patience by actually playing along for a bit. People don't get married in heaven, those who make it to heaven are more like angels than persons here on earth, and so on. But then he drops the big one: "He is God not of the dead, but of the living."[2] Stop screwing around—what I'm about is not what happens after you die. It's about a transformed life right now. As Jesus says provocatively on another occasion, "let the dead bury their own dead."[3] And if you are tired of being spiritually dead while physically alive, stop playing games and follow me.

Jesus does not promise that our bewilderment with the confusing and challenging aspects of our daily human existence will dissipate, but rather

---

1. Luke 20:27–38.
2. Luke 20:38.
3. Luke 9:60.

that we will find a source of peace, centeredness, meaning, and inspiration in the midst of a frequently difficult world. If we are to be the bearers of the divine into that world, we cannot be exclusively preoccupied with what happens once we are no longer in the world. Eternal life is a wonderfully attractive promise—even more attractive is that it begins now. In the middle of a world that often seems too much to take we bring the good news that God is with us, bearing every burden and enduring every pain that we are subject to. Faith does not provide a means of escape from the world, but rather of changing it.

There's nothing like unexpectedly dropping an f-bomb on a bunch of students. It's even better when one of them does it. I teach at a Catholic college, so one would think that the students would be used to talking about the f-word—we Baptists certainly were when I was growing up. But dropping an f-bomb in class, even when the context is entirely appropriate and the word is germane, is like farting in church. Everyone clams up, an uncomfortable atmosphere fills the room, and no one wants to deal with it. And I am presented with, as professors like to say, a "teachable moment."

Mark Twain once defined "faith" as "believing something you know ain't true." Strangely, I find that my largely parochial school educated students also think of faith in this way. Faith is opposed to reason, to logic, to evidence, yet is the foundation of what they have been told are the most important truths imaginable. Things believed by faith are certain and beyond question. But the above "facts" about faith are false. Far from being companions, faith and certainty are entirely incompatible. But that's not something I can just drop early into a conversation about the f-word. I have to build up to it.

A good place to start is with Anne Lamott's idea that faith is a verb, not a noun.[4] It's an activity, not a thing. So what exactly are we doing when we are "faithing"? I use a good technique that I learned in grammar school—"Someone use the word *faith* in a sentence that has absolutely nothing to do with religion, church, or God." Pretty soon someone says something like "I have faith that the chair I am sitting in will not collapse." Or "I have faith that the Red Sox will make the playoffs next year." I suggest, "I have faith that when the time comes, my friend John will make the right decision." All of these sentences are still treating faith as a noun rather than a verb, as

---

4. Tippett and Lamott, "The Meaning of Faith," line 437.

something you have rather than something you do, but progress is being made.

"Are you certain that the chair isn't going to collapse?" I ask. "Are you sure that the Red Sox will make the playoffs next year?" (especially since they have finished in last place in their division three of the last five seasons, with a world championship in one of the other seasons). "Well . . . no." So you're just guessing? Once again, "no." Apparently faithing is an activity that occupies the vast territory between certainty and guesswork—the knowledge territory in which we human beings spend a great deal of our time. Although my student can't prove that her chair won't collapse in the next minute, she can refer to past experience to support her faith claim—she's seen human beings in thousands of such chair situations in her life and has never seen a chair fail yet. Red Sox fans can point to the positive second half of the season after an embarrassingly abysmal first half, the promise of three or four brand new young players, a shake-up in upper management, and so on. My faith in my friend John is not blind; rather, it is based on years of observing his careful consideration of important alternatives before making a decision. When removed from the confines of religion, faithing turns out to be a perfectly natural activity—the activity of moving past evidence in hand toward a conclusion for which complete evidence is lacking. Faith is the activity of inching past probability toward something stronger (although the goal is never certainty).

With this in hand, we move to my go-to definition of faith: "Faith is the substance of things hoped for, the evidence of things not seen."[5] My good Catholic students who are largely ignorant of what the Bible contains are often surprised to find out that this is from the book of Hebrews, the first verse of Hebrews 11, which is sometimes called "the honor roll of faith." They are even more surprised to find that the definition says nothing about God, religion, heaven, hell, or any of the other accompanying items they are used to seeing in the entourage of a definition of faith. Instead, it is an excellent summary of what we have been discussing about faithing as a normal human activity. We faith when we want to provide substance to something important that we are hoping for (the chair will hold me up, the Red Sox will make the playoffs, my friend will make a good decision). All of the items hoped for are "unseen" because they either have not happened yet or cannot be proven true with certainty. Faithing fills in the gaps between

---

5. Heb 11:1.

evidence and what we hope for, realizing that further evidence over time may force us to adjust our hopes or discard them altogether.

In one of his letters, Rene Descartes tells the story of a king who refused to eat anything unless he could be convinced beyond the shadow of a doubt that it was not poisoned. And he starved to death. Some things—most things—cannot be established with certainty. Sometimes we just need to faith our way along. Faith in the realm of things divine is a case in point. I cannot know with certainty anything about God or even that God exists. But this does not mean that I am guessing or shutting down my brain when I faith. I can point to any number of past and present experiences that I count as evidence from which to take a faith leap in the direction of the divine. I can't prove it, but neither am I guessing.

In Milos Forman's 1984 Academy Award-winning film *Amadeus*, Holy Roman Emperor Joseph II, played by Jeffrey Jones of *Ferris Buehler's Day Off* fame, is an aspiring enlightened ruler who makes his decisions only after considering the advice of his cabinet entourage that accompanies him wherever he goes. Yet he is an emperor, so there is often uncertainty about how to interact with this very powerful "first among equals." Those who enter the emperor's presence often drop to one knee and kiss his hand, to which (after an appropriate few seconds of kissing) the emperor often responds by withdrawing his hand and saying "Please! Please! It's not a holy relic!" supported by the sycophantic chuckles of his surrounding posse.

The emperor is right—his hand isn't a holy relic—but it also isn't just a hand. When does a normal, everyday object become something more? When does the mundane become something special? Examples and possible answers abound. I have had frequent exposure to various aspects of the holy relic racket over the years teaching in Catholic higher education. I call it a racket because the whole idea of holy relics messes with my Protestant sensibilities, even though in the church of my youth we treated the Bible, which appears to be a mere book, with a reverence not to be outdone by the most dedicated Catholic holy relic aficionado. I remember, for instance, one summer when my cousin got turned in to the Bible camp authorities for moving a Bible from the seat of a glider swing and placing it on the grass nearby so he and I could operate the glider. I still remember the tone of voice with which the owner of the Bible yelled "*You put the Word of God on the ground!*" before making a beeline for the director's office.

One of my favorite ongoing assignments in my upper division classes is an intellectual notebook in which students are required to make at least two entries per week recording their reflection on and reactions to assigned readings and what is going on in class. One student a couple of years ago identified herself early in the semester as a "devout Catholic." Yet I could tell from the start that she had both the courage and the willingness to press her faith boundaries, which she did regularly in all sorts of ways. So I was a bit disappointed when in one of her last notebook entries of the semester she described in some detail a visit to a holy relic site while studying abroad in Rome the previous spring.

> I had the chance to visit Santa Croce in Gerusalemme where my class and I saw several Holy relics. Saint Helena, Constantine's mother, was sent to Jerusalem to bring back the holy relics of the passion of the Christ. She found parts of the cross that Jesus was crucified on but she wasn't exactly sure which cross was His. Saint Helena brought the crosses to an old, sick woman and placed each cross on top of her to see if she could identify the cross of Jesus. The woman was suddenly cured by the third cross. This cross now lies in Santa Croce as the cross of Jesus Christ along with several other holy relics such as the finger of St. Thomas which was placed in the wounds of the risen Christ, two thorns from Jesus' crown, a nail, and a nameplate which was nailed to the cross stating "Jesus of Nazareth."

Please, I thought. Are you kidding me? How can anyone take any of this seriously? I was reminded of Martin Luther, a vocal critic of the relic racket, who reportedly said that there were enough pieces of the true cross of Christ in the Europe of his day to have filled a German forest.

I was somewhat pleased to read further and discover that my student apparently had not needed to take my class to at least think a little bit critically.

> How much of these stories do I believe 100% to be true? . . . Who wrote this story down and why should they be a credible source? . . . Maybe someone planted all of these relics. Maybe they knew that as human beings we need concrete proof to believe. Maybe it was God planting these relics for us to find as the ultimate concrete proof that Jesus is the messiah—I don't know. I don't know.

Faith—Dealing with the "F" Word

Well *I* know, I thought. This stuff is all bullshit. I grew out of the idea that the Bible is a holy relic and the inerrant Word of God. You'll grow out of this.

My student concluded her notebook reflection with the following:

> What I do know is that there was a feeling that came across me that is very hard to describe. There was a silence amongst all of us in the small room of Santa Croce as if the Holy Spirit was present right in front of our eyes. My heart dropped. I knew I was breathing but did not feel like I was in control of my breaths. I was frozen and soon felt a rush come over me like I wanted to cry. I did not ask myself "Is this real?" I knew it was real. This must have been my faith taking control of my body. It was exciting. I cannot say whether the historical facts of what I learned that day are accurate or not. It doesn't matter, because I took away more than just a history lesson. I believe this is what the Holy Spirit wanted when guiding the writings of the gospel—a personal and unique experience.

In my comments I wrote "This is a very powerful paragraph, describing what my family would call a 'Big Bird moment.' This is something to remember and embrace. Don't ever forget it."

In the Gospel of John, Jesus compares the activity of the Spirit to the wind, which "blows where it chooses, and you hear the sound of it, but you do not know where it comes from or where it goes."[6] There is a wonderful, holy randomness to all of this, unpredictable so that it cannot be packaged or formalized, and so powerful that it cannot be mistaken or forgotten. Sacredness infuses everything, and anything can become a direct channel of the divine wind. Even random pieces of wood and bone.

The writing coach at a conference I attended once told us to "write what you would love to find." That's great advice—but of course that means the prospective writer has to do a lot of reading. At least I do, since I often don't know what I would "love to find" until I find it. Recently I stumbled across two such books on the recommendations of a couple of close friends.

The first suggestion came from a friend and colleague who occupies the office directly across the hall from mine. We know each other well; we have taught on an interdisciplinary faculty team together and have frequently talked about pedagogical issues. He brings his sons to his office on

---

6. John 3:8.

occasion—they like to peek into my office to see my collection of penguin stuff. And he reads my blog. One morning not long ago he said "I'm reading a book you would like; it's called *My Bright Abyss*. Christian Wiman is a poet, but this is sort of a spiritual memoir. It's tough reading at times, but he writes about the sort of things you write about." On his recommendation I ordered the book from Amazon.

One of the many things I love to find is well-trampled territory described as if the author just discovered it for the first time.

> Faith steals upon you like dew: some days you wake and it is there. And like dew, it gets burned off in the rising sun of anxieties, ambitions, distractions.[7]

I call myself a "person of faith" regularly, but that makes faith sound like something that, once the decision is made, is a regular part of one's daily apparel like shoes or underwear. But faith is much more ephemeral than that. When Jesus asks Peter, whom he has just rescued from drowning at the end of Peter's ill-fated effort to walk on water, "You of little faith, why did you doubt?"[8] I'm hoping Peter answered (or at least thought) "Because I'm a human being and this faith thing is like a magic trick: Now you see it, now you don't."

Wiman also rejects the notion of finding comfort in religious belief. My students often suggest that "comfort" is the main attraction of faith commitment: comfort that "all things work together for good" and comfort that in an afterlife "everything will work out." The next time I hear that in a classroom discussion (or anywhere else), I'll read this from *My Bright Abyss*:

> Christ is a shard of glass in your gut. Christ is God crying *I am here*, and here not only in what exalts and completes and uplifts you, but here in what appalls, offends, and degrades you, here in what activates and exacerbates all that you would call not-God. To walk through the fog of God toward the clarity of Christ is difficult because of how unlovely, how "ungodly" that clarity often turns out to be.[9]

Imagine if Jesus had said that "following me will be like a shard of glass in your gut." How many followers would that have attracted? Come to think of

---

7. Wiman, *Bright Abyss*, 93.
8. Matt 14:31.
9. Wiman, *Bright Abyss*, 121.

Faith—Dealing with the "F" Word

it, though, the Gospels claim that Jesus said many things like that. We just tend to ignore them.

The other book I loved finding came my way when the rector of the Episcopal church I attend, a good friend who is the closest thing I have to a spiritual director, asked if I had ever read *Learning to Walk in the Dark* by Barbara Brown Taylor. "I want to get it for you," she said, "but the last time I got you a book you already had it." I had not read any of Taylor's work; not wanting to undermine my friend's intended generosity but taking her suggestion seriously, I read three of Taylor's other books over the next few weeks. Not only have I found another literary soul mate, Jeanne is reading these books as well.

Taylor's *Leaving Church* is her memoir of how tending for her own spiritual health and growth required her leaving the active Episcopal priesthood, a story that I resonated with at many points. Her treatment of suffering and the book of Job in *An Altar in the World* was unforgettable, beginning with her description of why pain and suffering are not logical puzzles to be solved or abstract challenges to faith to be overcome.

> Pain is so real that less-real things like who you thought you were and how you meant to act can vanish like drops of water flung on a hot stove. Your virtues can become as abstract as algebra, your beliefs as porous as clouds.[10]

I have for the most part been mercifully free in my life thus far from the sort of paralyzing pain that she is describing and I am not confident that the faith I care about and profess would mean much of anything in the face of such pain. But her directness and honesty is unusual and much appreciated from a priest and theologian.

What would I like to find (and what am I interested in writing)? Anne Lamott is right—the answer is often the same to both questions. A friend and colleague asked not long ago who the audience is for what I write. I couldn't believe it when I answered "I guess my audience is people like me." I write for people who might resonate, as I do, with Christian Wiman's analogy for the life of faith:

> To live in faith is to live like the Jesus lizard, quick and nimble on the water into which a moment's pause would make it sink.[11]

---

10. Taylor, *Altar*, 164.
11. Wiman, *Bright Abyss*, 164.

It is a scene so familiar in our imaginations that it has become iconic. In films, on television, the subject of countless artistic renditions, we are transported back 2,000 years. It is a beautiful, cloudless day. Hundreds, perhaps thousands, of people have gathered in the countryside from miles around; some have walked for hours. On the top of a hill in the middle of the impromptu gathering is the man everybody has been talking about and has gathered to check out. In spite of the stories that seem to pop up everywhere this guy goes, you would not have been able to pick him out of a crowd. Then he opens his mouth, and the world is forever changed.

> Blessed are the poor in spirit, for theirs is the kingdom of heaven.
>
> Blessed are those who mourn, for they will be comforted.
>
> Blessed are the meek, for they will inherit the earth.
>
> Blessed are those who hunger and thirst for righteousness, for they will be filled.
>
> Blessed are the merciful, for they will receive mercy.
>
> Blessed are the pure in heart, for they will see God.
>
> Blessed are the peacemakers, for they will be called children of God.
>
> Blessed are those who are persecuted for righteousness' sake, for theirs is the kingdom of heaven.
>
> Blessed are you when people revile you and persecute you and utter all kinds of evil against you falsely on my account.
>
> Rejoice and be glad, for great is your reward in heaven.[12]

We don't know the details of the setting, of course—the traditional images are evocations of centuries of imagination. Maybe it was a cloudy and windy day. Maybe these words were spoken inside someone's home or a synagogue. Maybe they were shared in private with only a few intimate friends and confidants. Maybe the man never spoke these words at all and they are intended as a brief summary, written decades after the fact, of how he lived and called others to live. But the Beatitudes, the opening lines of Jesus' Sermon on the Mount in Matthew's gospel account, are so beautifully poetic, so rich yet sparse, so gentle yet powerful, so all-encompassing and embracing that over the centuries they have seeped into the Christian ethos as the summary expression, as the "mission statement" if you will, of a religion and all it professes to stand for. In many ways the Beatitudes are as familiar as the Lord's Prayer and the Twenty-Third Psalm—and this is unfortunate. For the beauty and familiarity of the language can easily disguise

---

12. Matt 5:1–11.

what is most remarkable about the Beatitudes—they are a crystal-clear call to radically uproot everything we think we know about value, about what is important, about prestige, about power, and even about God. They are a challenge to fundamentally change the world.

In God's economy, *none* of our assumptions can be relied upon and none of our common sense arrangements work. God's values are apparently the very opposite of those produced by our natural human wiring. Throughout the rest of the Sermon on the Mount, and consistently throughout virtually everything attributed to Jesus in the Gospels, the point is driven home. God is most directly found in the poor, the widows, the orphans, those for whom pretensions of being something or having influence are unavailable. The Gospels are clear that the one thing guaranteed to make God angry is to ignore such persons. Because in truth we *all* are impoverished, we *all* are abandoned, we *all* are incapable of taking care of ourselves, let alone anyone else. The poor, widows, and orphans simply no longer have the luxury of pretending otherwise.

Although it is tempting to imagine a social structure infused with the energy of the Beatitudes, they are not about transformed social institutions. They are about a transformational way of being in the world. The Beatitudes are far more than a beautifully poetic literary statement. They are the road map for how to carry our faith into the real world. The world we live in is no more naturally attuned to the challenge of the Beatitudes than was the world in which they were first spoken. Individuals infected with the energy of the Beatitudes are those whose responsibility it is to help transform reality. As Annie Dillard puts it, "God's works are as good as we make them."[13] The Beatitudes are a call to get to work.

---

13. Dillard, *Holy*, 47.

8

Prayer—What Are You Going to Do About It?

The trouble about God is that he is like a person who never acknowledges one's letters and so, in time, one comes to the conclusion either that he does not exist or that you have got the address wrong.[1] —Letter from C. S. Lewis to his brother

The dynamic of how to express what you want and how to guarantee that it actually happens has been on my radar ever since I can remember. I was born into a world in which preference expression was a highly evolved art form with the highest stakes imaginable. This high-stakes art form is called prayer. Prayer was so important that it took up significant space in every Sunday church gathering. There was even a middle of the week evening meeting dedicated specifically to the fine-tuning and honing of the art form—Wednesday night prayer meeting. As a creative youngster, I usually was able to find something in every foray to church to pique my interest, however briefly. I liked some of the hymns we sang on Sunday morning and evening, for instance, and enjoyed the stories in Sunday school. But we didn't sing on Wednesday nights—people gave testimonies, and then we prayed. For a very, very, *very* long time.

1. Lewis, *Yours*, 7.

Prayer—What Are You Going to Do About It?

I remember prayers that were more like speeches than anything else, insistent, complaining sorts of speeches whose intent was apparently to wear God down. Many of the prayers I heard as a child were detailed, extended laundry lists of things the pray-er wanted to have happen. Not that the things being asked for were unimportant—"please bring X to a saving knowledge of you," "please heal Y of diabetes," "please help Z find a job"—but the tone was often strange, petulantly childish, demanding, insinuating that this time, for once, God had damn well better get off his ass and do something. Of course anyone actually saying that at Wednesday prayer service would have been in danger of hellfire. Some people were known to be "prayer warriors"—our next-door neighbor was one of them—an unfortunate turn of phrase because from it I learned early on that the spiritual life is a struggle, involving warfare and all of the characteristics that define a good soldier. A prayer warrior, it seemed to me, was someone who could pray for longer periods of time and more loudly than others, but one earned this title only if a few, or even one, of one's prayers had apparently been answered at some point.

When prayer is packaged in this way, God becomes the ultimate wizard behind the curtain and our petitions become transactional. You do this for me and I'll do this for you. This conception of a prayer-answering God has a solid pedigree—the book we considered to be literally true includes many passages in which the wizard clearly invites the reader to ask for things, to express her heart's desire, to "call upon Me and I will answer you." I was reminded of this on a daily basis during my sabbatical a number of years ago when I joined a group of Benedictine monks three times a day for Psalm reading and prayer. Every human emotion imaginable is on display in the Psalms; sometimes, the psalmist is simply pissed because God has not been paying sufficient attention to their important requests and demands. If you ever want to get bummed out, to wonder what on earth God is up to, drop in on any Psalm in the 50 to 60 range and experience the silence and absence of God along with the psalmist. In virtually every one of these Psalms, something has gone wrong and the psalmist is looking for answers.

My best friend betrayed me—what are you going to do about it?

Wicked people are prospering—what are you going to do about it?

My life is not working out the way I want it to—what are you going to do about it?

People I know are sick and need healing—what are you going to do about it?

Someone I love has been treated unfairly—what are you going to do about it?

Most of these Psalms end with an "I will worship and praise you anyways" sort of final verse, but such verses don't sound particularly sincere. There is an energy and anger throughout that reminds me of Ruby Turpin in Flannery O'Connor's short story "Revelation," who, when her expectations concerning God have been disappointed one too many times, shakes her fist at the sky and shouts "*Who Do You Think You Are?*"[2] It's a place at which everyone who believes in the goodness of God will eventually arrive. And it's all a matter of disappointed expectations. If God is God, why is this happening? If I can't depend on God to be there when expected, to set things right when I don't approve of them, to punish the wicked and reward the just, what's the point of believing? What's the difference between a God who cannot be detected, understood, explained, or relied upon and no God at all?

These questions are the gateway to what one of my students in a colloquium in which we explored these issues a few years ago told me the course had challenged her to develop: *a more nuanced and interesting faith.* There is abundant evidence that runs counter to the relatively simplistic divine model that many of us were taught to believe in, the model of a problem-solving, prayer-answering God who can be manipulated into acting by the proper procedures and pious intentions. A more nuanced and interesting faith, a faith that gets the believer out of the spiritual nursery and into the arena of encounter with something far more challenging and disturbing, is a faith that neither ignores contrary evidence nor gives up on belief at the first sign of trouble. The question is, do I *want* to believe in a God I can't predict or control, a God who refuses to behave in the manner I would prefer? As Thomas Cahill asks in *The Gifts of the Jews*, "Can we open ourselves to the God who cannot be understood, who is beyond all our amulets and scheming, the God who rains on picnics, the God who allows human beings to be inhuman, who has sentenced all of us to death?"[3] Opening up to that sort of God requires both guts and a willingness to continually readjust and retool. But it is certainly interesting.

Are we only talking to ourselves in an empty universe? The silence is

---

2. O'Connor, *The Complete Stories*, 507.
3. Cahill, *The Gifts*, 86.

Prayer—What Are You Going to Do About It?

often so emphatic. And we have prayed so much already.[4] —C. S. Lewis

I learned to play the prayer game, but my heart was never in it. I observed that most of the preferences expressed were never satisfied and often wondered what the point of expressing always unanswered petitions was in the first place. Constitutionally I couldn't take prayer seriously, simply because I wasn't convinced that I was important enough for God to push my wishes to the top of the divine to-do list. How to pray was a mystery to me—I recall my mother saying frequently that I should just "talk to God the same way you talk to me." That never struck me as one of my mother's better pieces of advice, since I clearly *couldn't* talk to an invisible, faraway, scary "something" in the same way I could talk to her. But I did learn, as all good Baptist kids learned, how to make up a convincing sounding prayer at the drop of a hat. It's just that it never seemed to go past the ceiling.

Remnants of my Baptist upbringing reared their head the first time I saw the Episcopal *Book of Common Prayer*. The whole idea of written, non-spontaneous prayer was foreign to me, despite the beauty of many of the petitions in the book. Over time I've gotten used to the idea of canned and ready-to-use prayer, though, since I've spent my working career with people trained in the "prepared prayer" camp. As the chair and only non-Catholic in a large philosophy department several years ago, for instance, it was one of my many ongoing tasks to ask a colleague to open our monthly department meetings with prayer. I was expected, of course, to ask the professionals, one of my priest colleagues, so I took great delight in occasionally asking a lay colleague just before the meeting if he (the only women in the department were a nun and a former nun) would assume the opening prayer duty. Without fail, you would have thought I had asked the colleague to solve several problems in differential calculus on the spot—apparently Catholics aren't used to praying on a moment's notice, with priests in the room and no prepared text at hand.

My overall attitude about prayer over the years has been, sad to say, an angry one. Prayer is supposed to be such a central part of the life of faith, but the transactional model I had been taught revealed God to be either arbitrary, powerless, uninterested, or hard of hearing. Anger and prayer are not necessarily opposed; as Ernest Kurtz and Katherine Ketcham observe, "There is an affinity between cursing and praying . . . both forms of discourse address what is out of human control: one with a destructive

---

4. Lewis, *Letters*, 61.

and the other with a creative purpose. Both praying and cursing flow from frustration."[5] But angry prayer doesn't do much to establish a prayer life with one's spouse, especially a spouse who, like Jeanne, seems to take to prayer as naturally as a duck to water. One day after expressing my frustration about the whole prayer thing to her, Jeanne said something that, for the first time, began to chip away at my icy attitude about talking to God. "Vance," she said, "for you thinking is praying." That was the most helpful thing anyone has ever said to me about prayer and, in turn, it freed me to learn what else prayer might be.

Among the writers who have been most important to me over the past several years, there turns out to be an amazing consensus about what prayer is and is not. It definitely is not begging, asking, bartering, transactional, or projecting religious white noise into the void. Rather, it has to do with openness, with waiting, with an attentiveness that does not fill in the silence but is, to use a phrase favored by contemporary philosophers, "fearlessly passive." Experiencing Benedictine communal prayer over the past few years has helped me with this. There is more silence than speaking in their petitions, sandwiched between the lines of the Psalms that we read together and between each portion of the rubric. I've heard "Be still and know that I am God"[6] since my childhood, but finding myself a part of it in action was a revelation.

As a new attitude of attention developed, it slowly became possible to return to spoken prayer without all of my previous baggage. Yet for the most part, prayer is an attitude rather than something verbal, an attitude that begins with finding the silent space inside. Some days are tougher than others, the sorts of days when "Help!" is the only appropriate prayer. But when Jeanne said to me a while ago that my prayers weren't angry any more, I was both thankful and aware that a change had indeed begun.

"Writing is prayer," Kafka, that most afflicted one, said. And writing, certainly, isn't wishing; it is witnessing.[7] —Patricia Hampl

Over the past several years I have learned more about prayer indirectly and from unexpected sources than from "experts" (if there is such a thing as an "expert" in communicating with the divine). One of these unexpected

5. Kurtz and Ketcham, *Spirituality*, 220.
6. Ps 46:10.
7. Hampl, *I Could Tell*, 164.

sources is Reverend John Ames from Marilynne Robinson's beautiful and Pulitzer Prize-winning novel *Gilead*. It is as close to perfect as any book I have read. Ames is a Congregational minister in Iowa; he is in his late seventies and writing a memoir for his young son, an only child unexpectedly born to Reverend Ames and his much-younger wife when Ames is seventy. Ames expects to die long before the child is grown, and *Gilead* is his love letter to his son containing as much guidance and wisdom as Ames can muster. The prose is serenely beautiful. Ames writes that for him "writing has always felt like praying, even when I wasn't writing prayers, as I was often enough. You feel that you are with someone."[8] On my best writing days I have this in mind as a standard. Join this with Jeanne's insight that for me thinking is prayer, along with the hopeful possibility that careful reading might also be prayer, and maybe I'm in better shape on this prayer thing than I thought.

I don't remember how *Gilead* came to me, but Ames's struggles with the austere doctrine of his Calvinist faith are familiar. His is the religious world of my youth, a world that I have struggled mightily at different times to understand, to incorporate, or to leave. One passage in particular shook me to my core:

> Calvin says somewhere that each of us is an actor on a stage and God is the audience. That metaphor has always interested me, because it makes us artists of our behavior, and the reaction of God to us might be thought of as aesthetic rather than morally judgmental in the ordinary sense. How well do we understand our role? With how much assurance do we perform it? . . . We all bring such light to bear on these great matters as we can. I do like Calvin's image, though, because it suggests how God might actually enjoy us. I believe we think about that far too little.[9]

The simple image of God as the audience for the artistic performance of the human drama and comedy, rather than the authoritative judge who is taking note of every single one of our failures, has been transformative for me. I remember the exact moment several years ago when, during a noonday reading of daily psalms, we read in Psalm 149 that "the Lord takes pleasure in his people."[10] This verse has turned out to be one of the most welcome, yet shocking, lines in the Bible for me. I grew up in a world overseen by a

---

8. Robinson, *Gilead*, 19.
9. Ibid., 124.
10. Ps 149:4.

stern and judgmental God, a being of whom I was both afraid and whose job description was far too lofty to be concerned about someone as insignificant as me, except when I did something wrong—then all bets were off. So I tried to go under the radar screen as much as possible. But if God takes pleasure in me, then perhaps God is not looking for me to be the lowest of the low-maintenance. My preferences matter, not because I have any particular insight into what is best, but simply because they are mine. I left the transactional God who might give me what I want if I beg or petition often or strongly enough behind a number of years ago. I have no reason to believe that any given thing I ask for will happen. But I do believe that there is something greater than me and I do believe that my input is invited by whatever that something greater is. Where I fall on the high to low maintenance spectrum with regard to prayer tells me little about God but it tells me a lot about myself. I may not be important enough to get everything (or anything) that I want, but I am important enough to say something. And perhaps be heard.

The essence of prayer is a song and men cannot live without a song. Prayer may not save us, but prayer may make us worthy of being saved. Prayer is not requesting. There is a partnership of God and men. God needs our help.[11] —Rabbi Abraham Joshua Heschel

A few summers ago I spent five days silent retreating at a Benedictine hermitage in Big Sur. Time spent in Benedictine atmosphere offers the opportunity to plug into the daily cycle of Psalms and prayers that has been going on for over fifteen hundred years. Something deep in me resonates with its rhythms. One particular foggy morning, bright and early at 5:30 Vigils, Psalm 5 began as a cry for someone, anyone, to listen.

> Give ear to my words, O Lord,
> give heed to my sighing.
> Listen to the sound of my cry,
> my King and my God.[12]

---

11. Tippett and Eisen, *Spiritual Audacity*, lines 298-302.
12. Ps 5:1-3.

Prayer—What Are You Going to Do About It?

As so often with the Psalms, the psalmist has a story to tell and insists that it be heard. And so it goes with all of us; the stories that define and shape us, that clothe the bare facts of our lives in fancy dress, are only the sound of one hand clapping unless there is someone to receive the story on the other end.

My early story was enriched by the presence of all four grandparents during my formative years. Visiting my paternal grandparents was always an event that took several days of careful and intense planning. We lived in northeastern Vermont; they lived on the outskirts of Erie, Pennsylvania, still in the house that my father grew up in. It was an almost 600-mile trip, with the first 200 on narrow two-lane roads before finally hitting the New York Thruway headed west, so some serious entertainment planning on my brother's and my part and food packing on my mother's part for the trip was always in order. My grandfather worked for General Electric, wrapping the coils in the back of old-time refrigerators by hand around a mold. He had forearms like Popeye—one of his favorite parlor tricks was to bet someone that he could make them close their hand just by squeezing their wrist in his vice-like grip. He never lost the bet.

Grandma was loving and had a great sense of humor, but also was noisy and abrupt, sort of like my dad, and was a horrible cook. I don't remember any item of food—meat, vegetable, fruit, or starch—that my grandmother could not reduce to tasteless pulp after what seemed like endless hours sweating and complaining in the kitchen. But she sure could dish up ice cream. Her signature dessert, usually served in the early evening in front of some mindless thing on television, was to open a half-gallon carton of vanilla ice cream, cut it in quarters with a knife so large that my brother and I were warned upon pain of serious comeuppance (one of her favorite words) to stay away from it, then serve a quarter to each person in the room with so much chocolate sauce and so many peanuts slathered on top that one would forget that there was vanilla ice cream underneath. This, of course, was before healthy eating habits were invented. A dessert designed to make one forget the less-than-palatable meal that preceded it.

The Erie homestead was nothing special, just old with creepy and creaky bedrooms upstairs. My other grandparents' home in the Finger Lakes region of southern New York State was far more interesting and "homey," probably because that set of grandparents was more touchy-feely and grandparently than my dad's folks. But the fun of going to Erie was not the house—the fun wasn't really even my grandparents. What made Erie a favored point of destination was that my grandfather, in addition to being a blue-collar factory laborer, was also a "city farmer." Stretched behind their house on a busy road in what served as suburbia in the early 1960s was two acres of land upon which my grandfather ran a small farm, complete with a barn, horse, cow, chickens, tons of barn cats, an outhouse, a huge vegetable garden, a dozen long rows of grape vines, and a lower field where hay always seemed to be growing unnoticed. My other grandfather was the real farmer who made a living growing fields of potatoes, but my gentleman farmer grandfather in Erie is the man of the soil I remember most clearly. When I take delight in digging around in the flower beds, pruning bushes, watering things and watching them grow, I am channeling my Grandpa Morgan.

In addition to their farm animal menagerie, my grandparents had a dog named King. King died of old age before I was ten years old, but if he actually looked as I remember him, he was probably a collie/shepherd mix of some sort. We had two dogs at home, a collie named Lassie, and Rex, our German Shepherd; if they had ever mated (which they didn't), their offspring might have looked something like King. King could do two things that neither of my dogs could do. For starters, King was the first dog I ever met who would chase a ball and bring it back to you over and over again until your arm got too tired to throw any more. At home, if you threw a ball for Lassie to chase she would look at you with a "You're kidding, right?" sort of look as she laid down, and a ball thrown in Rex's direction would most likely bounce off his head. I thought King was a genius with his ball retrieval abilities and should be on the Ed Sullivan show; it wasn't until much later that I learned ball retrieval is a normal dog activity and that my dogs at home were just strange.

King's other trick was vocal in nature. My grandfather or my dad would say "Tell me a big story, King, tell me a big story!" in a certain tone of voice and King would immediately raise his snout heavenward and start howling up a storm. The story King told was sad and full of pathos, dramatic and primal, with the mournful tones of his wolf ancestors. But King was selective about who he would tell his stories to. Only my grandfather or dad would do. In response to such requests from my grandmother, my mother, my brother, me, or any of my aunts and uncles who lived in the area, King would stare in mute silence. King's stories were meant only for the chosen few, those who knew how to ask properly.

Prayer—What Are You Going to Do About It?

Our best and most important stories should be, and usually are, saved for the ears of those who deserve them. Because woven into every story worth the telling is the intended listener. A story is far more than a linear reporting of facts; by fashioning facts into a narrative the storyteller reveals a great deal about who he or she is as well as about what he or she considers to be of ultimate importance. In Yann Martel's *Life of Pi*, responding to a demand for nothing but the facts about what has happened, Pi responds that

> a story always has an element of *invention* in it . . . . Isn't telling about something—using words, English or Japanese—already something of an invention? Isn't just looking upon the world already something of an invention? The world isn't just the way it is. It is how we understand it, no? And in understanding something, we bring something to it, no? Doesn't that make life a story?"[13]

Yes, it does. And by sending his cries and groans heavenward, the psalmist is weaving a fascinating character into his story—a God who listens. This is my hope as a person of faith, that there is not only something greater than me, but something that knows me better than I know myself, that listens, and promises a response. Sound like a fictional character, someone from mythology? I hope so, because as a wise person once said, a myth is a story that you know is true the first time you hear it. By including God in my story, I create a space in which God can show up.

When the minister finally got to say his "Let us pray," we were ready. We had been praying, all along. We had been being ourselves before God.[14]
— Kathleen Norris

---

13. Martel, *Life of Pi*, 302.
14. Norris, *Cloister Walk*, 282.

9

Courage—I'll Remember You

On a beautiful, crystal clear June afternoon I sat in an alpine meadow at the foot of the spectacularly majestic Grand Tetons in northwestern Wyoming. A handful of family was gathered to pay final respects to and spread the ashes of my father, who had died a few months earlier. On the porch of my brother's house that morning, I had considered what Scripture text might be appropriate to read as we honored a man who had memorized massive amounts of Scripture in his lifetime, a man whose life and teaching had been a catalyst of liberation in the lives of many for whom the traditional church no longer gave life, and with whom I had maintained a tenuously "okay" relationship for most of my life. Sitting on a rock in the afternoon sun next to my son Justin, who could barely keep his emotions in check, I read the following passage from Isaiah, verses that had jumped off the page through my tears that morning:

> The Spirit of the Lord God is upon me,
> because the Lord has anointed me;
> he has sent me to bring good news to the oppressed,
> to bind up the brokenhearted,
> to proclaim liberty to the captives,
> and release to the prisoners . . . .[1]

---

1. Isa 61:1.

Courage—I'll Remember You

Scholars tell us that these verses are prophetic of the Messiah to come, but my father would have embraced this text as descriptive of his own courageous calling, particularly to "proclaim liberty" to persons whose lives had been derailed or ruined by organized religion. As I choked my way through the reading on that summer afternoon, I knew that "Mad Eagle," as we sometimes called him when he wasn't around, would have approved.

An early text in Luke's gospel reprises the passage from Isaiah that I read at my father's memorial service. Jesus is fresh off his forty days and nights of temptation in the desert and returns to Nazareth, his hometown. What better place to kick off his ministry? The scene is powerfully portrayed in the 1977 Franco Zeffirelli television miniseries *Jesus of Nazareth*. It is the Sabbath, and Jesus is in the synagogue with wall-to-wall men and boys, while the women of the town, including Jesus' mother, observe from behind a screen. Although it is apparently not his turn to read, Jesus steps to the front and takes the scroll. After a pregnant pause, he begins to read. "The Spirit of the Lord is upon me, because he has anointed me to preach good tidings to the poor...."[2] When he is finished, Jesus rolls up the scroll, makes eye contact with the congregation, and says "Today this scripture has been fulfilled in your hearing."[3]

As the camera slowly pans the faces of those at the synagogue, their expressions pass from piety, to confusion, then to outrage and anger. For every man and woman present knows that this Scripture can only be fulfilled by the Messiah. They also know who this man is. He is Mary and Joseph's son. He is a carpenter—a bit odd at times, ordinary just as they are. Nazareth is an insignificant town in an insignificant backwater of the eastern Roman Empire. "I remember when I chased you out of my bakery for stealing a fig," one thinks. "I remember when I had to break up a squabble between you and my son when you were teenagers," thinks another. "I remember that you were attracted to my daughter but never approached me concerning betrothal," thinks a third. And this guy has just declared himself to be the son of God. No wonder they tried to kill him.

Christians believe that, despite the understandable incredulity of his fellow worshipers on that Sabbath, Jesus was indeed the Messiah, God in flesh. Remarkable and astounding. But even more remarkable is that these twenty-five-hundred-year-old words from Isaiah were not only fulfilled by Jesus—they continue to be fulfilled by God in human form.

2. Luke 4:18.
3. Luke 4:21.

Isaiah's prophecy foretells a time when healing, justice and liberation will be brought to the sick, oppressed and prisoners. That time is *now*, and *we* are the vehicles of that healing, justice, and liberation. Our world is full of the poor, the bound, those who mourn, those who are in captivity both physically and mentally. We live in a world crying out for liberation, peace, and consolation at every level. So often we wonder where God is, where the divine solution to the never-ending problems and tragedies of our world is to be found.

But we miss the clear answer to our questions. Joan Chittister writes that

> Having made the world, having given it everything it needs to continue, having brought it to the point of abundance and possibility and dynamism, God left it for us to finish. God left it to us to be the mercy and the justice, the charity and the care, the righteousness and the commitment, all that it will take for people to bring the goodness of God to outweigh the rest.[4]

We are to be the oil of joy for those who mourn, to be the beauty in the midst of ashes, and to wrap the heavy of heart in the garment of praise. As the closing prayer in each eucharistic celebration in the Episcopal liturgy asks, "Send us now into the world in peace, and grant us strength and courage to love and serve you with gladness and singleness of heart."[5]

A Polish Franciscan priest. A Lutheran pastor and theologian. A French-Jewish social activist attracted to Marxism. A French novelist and philosopher. A group of young German college students. The citizens of an isolated rural town in France. What do the above persons have in common? In unique and profound ways, Maximillian Kolbe, Dietrich Bonhoeffer, Simone Weil, Albert Camus, the members of the White Rose, and the people of Le Chambon were witnesses to the power of the human spirit and the dignity of the human person in the face of unimaginable horror and atrocity. And these were the figures that we studied in my team-taught colloquium—"'Love Never Fails': Grace, Truth, and Freedom in the Nazi Era" during the second half of a recent semester.

In the first half of the colloquium, my colleague and I delved deeply with our students into the darkest features of the Nazi years. Perhaps even

---

4. Chittister and Williams, *Uncommon Gratitude*, 191.
5. *Book of Common Prayer*, 365.

more disturbing than the horrors they perpetuated were the various techniques people used to collaborate with, to deliberately turn away from, and to ignore evil—even with partial or full knowledge of the atrocities being committed. As we then considered examples of persons who did otherwise, responding directly through words and actions to what was happening all around them, we found that the motivations for and manners of response were as varied as those responding. Some had religious motivations, while the response of others was political in nature. Some lost their lives, while the activities of others were protected by distance and obscurity.

For the last seminar of the semester, I gave my eighteen students the following in-class assignment: suppose, based on what we have learned this semester, that we wanted to write a handbook or guide for future generations on how to preserve and perpetuate goodness in the midst of evil. Are there any common techniques or skills that the people we studied this semester invariably relied on as they responded to evil? The students worked on this in small groups for twenty minutes or so, then reported back to the larger group with their results. In no particular order, here are some of my students' suggestions concerning how to preserve one's character and integrity in the face of severe challenges.

Know who you are: One can quickly become overwhelmed by the apparently monumental task of facing up to systematic evil and wrongdoing. In such situations, the only reasonable response appears to be "What can I do? I am only one person—I can't make a difference." But we learned that moral character begins with understanding who I am and what I am capable of. I cannot change the world, but I can do something about what is right in front of me. Moral character does not require moral heroism or sainthood. Consider the story of the Good Samaritan, a story frequently referenced by various people we studied.[6] The Good Samaritan was just a guy on a trip who stumbled across an injustice that he could do something about. His response to the man dying in the ditch was not motivated by philosophy, religion, politics, or personal gain—it was simply a human response to human need. That not only is enough, it can be miraculous. As the Jewish saying goes, "he who saves one life saves the entire world."

Simplicity: One of my typical roles as a philosophy professor is convincing my students to dig deeper, because things are always more complicated than they seem. But one of the continuing themes of this semester was that those who respond effectively to evil and wrongdoing often reduced moral

---

6. Luke 10:30–37.

complexities to manageable proportions. The villagers of Le Chambon believed that human need must be addressed. Period. They also believed that all human life is precious, from Jewish refugees to Nazi officers. Period. The students of the White Rose believed that their country had been stolen from them and they had to help take it back. Period. Maximillian Kolbe lived his life believing that God, Jesus, and the Blessed Mother love everyone. Period. In response to complaints that "things aren't that simple," the consistent message during this semester was "sometimes they are."

Some things are more important than life. I have often asked students over the years "what things are worth dying for?" more or less as a thought experiment. But for the people we studied, this was not an academic exercise. In the early weeks of the semester we often saw people choosing not to act or turning the other way because they were afraid for their own lives. My students frequently were willing to give such persons at least a partial pass, arguing that self-preservation is the strongest instinct that human beings possess. Then we encountered a series of people who proved that not to be true. Just as Socrates sharply drew a contrast between "living" and "living well" more than two millennia ago, my students and I encountered a series of counterexamples to the notion that self-preservation trumps everything else. In a variety of ways, those who responded to evil demonstrated that some things are more important than guaranteeing one's continuing survival. Socrates argued that some lives are not worth living; a life preserved by refusing to do whatever one can to resist evil is one of those lives.

Spirituality: Any number of the persons we studied placed their understanding of themselves and the world around them within a framework that included something greater than us. My students chose to call this "spirituality" rather than "faith" or "religion," since many of the persons we studied were not religious in any traditional sense. But all were convinced that we human beings are answerable to something greater than ourselves; ideas about what that something is ranged from the divine to a responsibility to create a better future.

Look toward the other: One of the most important keys to preserving goodness in the presence of evil is the ability to focus my attention on something other than myself. Iris Murdoch defined love as "the extremely difficult realization that something other than oneself is real,"[7] and from the villagers of Le Chambon through Maximillian Kolbe to the students of the White Rose, my students and I encountered individuals who incor-

---

7. Murdoch, *Existentialists*, 215.

porated this ability into their daily lives. Thinkers and writers in all ages warn against falling prey to the temptations of the self. There is no greater technique for escaping these temptations than cultivating a sharp awareness of reality beyond myself.

Don't be afraid: In *The Plague*, Albert Camus suggests that most human evil is the result of ignorance. Although my students resonated with this notion, they concluded on the basis of their studies that in situations of moral emergency and stress, fear is a greater problem than ignorance. There is a reason why the first thing that an angel usually says in Scripture when unexpectedly dropping into someone's reality is "Fear not," since we often respond to the unknown, the strange, and the overwhelming with fear. The message of the human angels we studied together was "Don't be afraid to expose your small spark of goodness in a world of darkness. It might just change or save a life—perhaps yours."

Self-knowledge, simplicity, the ability to recognize what is truly important, spiritual awareness, courage—these are not magical moral weapons available only to saints and heroes. I can do this. You can do this. But only if we start now. Good habits can only be developed through repetition; we only become skillful wielding the weapons of the spirit through practice. Let's get started.

The first semester faculty in the interdisciplinary program I teach in have to make many tough choices. *Iliad* or *Odyssey*? What texts from the Hebrew Scriptures? The New Testament? And which of the triumvirate of great Greek tragedians? Usually it is a toss-up between the profundity of Sophocles and the brilliance of Euripides, but a couple of years ago my teammate and I opted for the first of the trio, Aeschylus. We spent a week with sixty-five freshmen in *The Oresteia*, a trilogy with enough violence and dysfunctional family intrigue to put a reality television show to shame. Perhaps some of the playwright's profound insights into the human condition seeped in as well.

In our current political climate, it is hard to imagine a candidate for national public office quoting from an ancient Greek tragedian. But on April 4 1968, a month after my twelfth birthday, presidential candidate Robert F. Kennedy quoted early lines from *Agamemnon*, the first play of Aeschylus's trilogy, toward the end of a brief, impromptu eulogy of Martin Luther King, Jr., who had been assassinated in Memphis earlier in the day. Kennedy, who would himself be killed by an assassin's bullet just two short months later, included these lines from the Chorus's first speech in the play as a sobering portion of one of the great speeches in American history:

> Even in our sleep, pain which cannot forget
> falls drop by drop upon the heart until,
> in our despair, against our will,
> comes wisdom through the awful grace of God.[8]

I was reminded of both Bobby Kennedy and these lines from Aeschylus as I was listening to *The Moth Radio Hour* on NPR not long ago.[9] One of the story-tellers at the Moth event was Sala Udin, who described how as a Freedom Rider in Mississippi fifty years ago he was stopped and then viciously beaten to within an inch of his life by the Mississippi State Police. In his jail cell, as he looked at his battered and disfigured face in the mirror, he realized that the police had made a mistake—they should have killed him. Because now he was committed to being a Freedom Rider for the rest of his life. Udin and thousands like him were some of those drops upon the heart that Aeschylus wrote of over two millennia ago. Because of persons like Udin, change in the direction of wisdom incrementally but inexorably comes "against our will," a change that although real is nowhere near complete.

I was born in 1956 and was too young to be directly involved in the early days of the civil rights movement, but have often wondered whether I would have had the courage to be a Freedom Rider if given the opportunity. I take a small amount of comfort in the belief that once the habit is developed, courage tends to be available in the amounts needed by present circumstances. Aristotle wisely says that if you want to be courageous, you should do the things that courageous people do. I have never been faced directly with having to answer with actions the question of what I would be willing to stake my life on and possibly die for, but can at least hope that faced with the decision to act on what things are worth risking or even losing my life for, I would not immediately run away.

Jeanne and I recently watched one of our favorite movies—*Amazing Grace*—with a good friend who had never seen it. The 2007 movie includes fine acting performances from various rising young actors who now are some of the hottest performers going—Ioan Gruffudd, Benedict Cumberbatch, Rufus Sewell, Romola Garai—the wonderful Ciaran Hinds, and two

---

8. Aeschylus, *Agamemnon*, lines 179–82.

9. Udin, "Freedom Rider," https://themoth.org/stories/i-want-to-be-a-freedom-rider.

of my favorite older actors, Michael Gambon and Albert Finney. *Amazing Grace* is the story of William Wilberforce's twenty-year political campaign to end the slave trade in England, finally accomplished in 1807 (the movie is a celebration of the bicentennial of that legislation). I have no idea how historically accurate the movie is, but as my good friend and colleague Rodney used to say, if it isn't true it should be. It's a great story.

Although there are certainly "good guys" and "bad guys" in *Amazing Grace*, no one is close to saintly or perfect. The dogged attempts of Wilberforce (played by Gruffudd) to end slavery meet with resistance for reasons that sound unfortunately familiar. Ending the slave trade will be devastating economically, there is "evidence" that the slaves in the colonies live better than the poor in England, non-whites in the colonies are "the white man's burden," as Rudyard Kipling will write decades later, and so on. As he encounters multiple defeats and disappointments, Wilberforce is on the brink of despair when he has a conversation with his childhood minister, John Newton (played by Finney). Before becoming a member of the clergy years earlier, Newton had been a successful captain of a slave ship; through various powerful and transformative experiences, he recognized the evil underlying his profession, and famously wrote a poem that he set to a familiar and popular tune. The result was "Amazing Grace," perhaps the most beloved song in the hymnal, in which the now-blind Newton wrote "I once was lost, but now am found; was blind, but now I see."

In the middle of their conversation, Newton mentions he has heard that Wilberforce is returning to the faith of his youth; Wilberforce confirms the rumor, but says that while he badly needs divine inspiration and help, there have been no inspirational lightning bolts thus far. "Ah," replies Newton, "but God sometimes does his work through gentle drizzle rather than storms." Many more years pass before Wilberforce and his supporting cohorts from all walks of life stumble upon a strategy that finally works, confirming Newton's insight. The frontal attacks of previous years, energized by righteous anger, eloquent statesmanship, and the best of moral intentions have failed again and again. It is not until an obscure lawyer in Wilberforce's entourage of like-minded persons suggests a new strategy— essentially "we cheat"—that success is finally gained. Through behind-the-scenes manipulation and the use of a long neglected, virtually unknown set of maritime regulations, Wilberforce does a brilliant end run on his political opponents and slavery in Great Britain soon crumbles under its own weight. It will take more than another half century and a brutal civil war for the same to happen in the United States.

"God sometimes does his work through gentle drizzle rather than storms." That certainly has been my experience, both in my own life and as I have observed the world around me for more than six decades. In its Latin roots, to "convert" means to "turn around," but this turning is more often like a sunflower following the sun in its slow course across the sky than a dynamic and once-for-all event. I am an optimist at heart, something that is often difficult to sustain when I think about how much there is to be accomplished in my own life and in the world around me. But a steady rain, even a gentle drizzle, is better for my plants and grass than an inch-and-a-half-hour downpour. Beneath the layers of violence, hatred, ignorance, and despair, something holy is lurking. Let the gentle drizzle and drops upon the heart release it.

Recently I led a seminar attended by twenty colleagues from the honors faculty. The text was a handful of essays from Montaigne's *Essais*; toward the end of a fine discussion we focused our attention on one of Montaigne's many memorable reflections, this one from the last page of his monumental work:

> The most beautiful of lives to my liking are those which conform to the common measure, human and ordinate, without miracles, though, and without rapture.[10]

My colleagues were not unanimous in their reaction to Montaigne's sentiment, but when are academics ever unanimous concerning anything? A few suggested that this was both a recipe for mediocrity and a denial of the importance of miracles and ecstasy. A colleague from my department said "Socrates would not have agreed with any of this," and I overheard another colleague close by grumble that Emily Dickinson would not have approved either. They are probably right, although I suspect that Montaigne did not have the approval of an Athenian from 2,000 years earlier or the approval of a New England spinster and recluse three centuries in the future at the top of his list of concerns as he wrote.

Other colleagues found much to approve of in this passage. A professor from the history department who had just finished the final year of an outstanding teaching and scholarly career said, "I find this inspiring. It says

---

10. Montaigne, *The Essays*, 426.

that a beautiful life is not to be judged by whether you get your name on a plaque in city hall." This from a man who has a seminar room in our beautiful new humanities center named after him in honor of his extraordinary contributions over several decades to thousands of students and hundreds of colleagues at our college.

I also find this passage from Montaigne to be inspirational. He is not suggesting that mountaintop experiences are unimportant; rather, he is reminding us that a beautiful life is not constructed from such experiences. There is a reason why the greatest portion of the liturgical year, although seasoned with the miracle of the incarnation and the rapture of Easter, is spent in long stretches of inwardness, waiting, and getting down to the day-to-day, week-to-week work of being a regular human being trying to live a life in the presence of the Divine. As the old saying says, life is what happens while we are making other plans. Montaigne suggests that the beauty of a life is to be judged by what you are doing between the miracles and the ecstasy.

Once Jeanne and I had brunch with two couples after church, a lovely occasion that we all agreed should happen more frequently. All six of us have been to a few rodeos—at fifty-nine I was the youngest person at the table. One of us had celebrated a birthday a week or so earlier, so we all sang happy birthday as the waiter brought her a small dessert. The waiter remarked on Jeanne's beautiful singing voice, a nice connection was made, and good vibes were in abundance. Jeanne and I tend to be generous with tips when the service is good; this time, Jeanne was so generous when bill-paying time came that the waiter returned with the cash, wondering if Jeanne had made a mistake. She assured him that she hadn't; we then learned he would be headed for Los Angeles in a month to pursue a career in entertainment promotion. Grabbing his hands, Jeanne offered a quick, heartfelt and spontaneous prayer asking for God's blessing on this young man's endeavors. "I'll remember you," he said to Jeanne as he headed back to the kitchen. And I'm sure he will—it was a lovely moment of grace in the midst of an ordinary Sunday afternoon.

The closing paragraph of George Eliot's *Middlemarch* is not only the most perfect paragraph I have read in any of the hundreds of novels in my reading life, but also is a perfect expression of the sort of life Montaigne recommends. Of her heroine Dorothea Brooke, Eliot writes:

> Her finely touched spirit had still its fine issues, though they were not widely visible. Her full nature, like that river of which Cyrus

broke the strength, spent itself in channels which had no great name on the earth. But the effect of her being on those around her was incalculably diffusive: for the growing good of the world is partly dependent on unhistoric acts; and that things are not so ill with you and me as they might have been, is half owing to the number who lived faithfully a hidden life, and rest in unvisited tombs.[11]

I would love to write a best seller. I would love to have my likeness be the first one carved on the Mount Rushmore for Teachers that someone should create sometime. I would love to have thousands of people all over the world waiting with rapt attention for my next wise and witty blog post. But I would like most to faithfully live a life according to Montaigne's "common measure," bringing what I have to offer into each new day with intelligence, energy, and an occasional infusion of divine humor. Miracles and rapture are fine if you get them, but at the end of the road a "nicely done" would be even better.

---

11. Eliot, *Middlemarch*, 794.

10

Humility—From Infinity to Intimacy

My youngest son was always the inquisitive sort, the kind of kid who, from the moment he began to speak, fashioned most of his communication into questions starting with the word "Why?" The setting for one of his favorite stories is the beat up car I was driving when he was three or four years old; I was running errands and he was strapped into the car seat next to me on the passenger's side facing the front. This was, as a friend of mine says, "before safety was invented."

On this particular day I apparently had only sufficient tolerance for one thousand "Whys" before noon. As soon as he asked his one thousand and first "Why?" I yelled *"Stop asking so many questions!"* To which, I'm sure, he replied "Why?" I have no recollection of this event, since it makes me look bad. But here's what *I* remember as my usual response when his litany of questions exceeded tolerable levels. After several consecutive "Dad, why . . . . ?" events, I would reply "I don't know, Justin—it must be a miracle."

And for a long time, that was an effective show stopper, because as Simone Weil wrote, "the stories about miracles confuse everything."[1] We want answers and explanations, and a miracle says "Oh, yeah? Explain *this*, jerk!" We can't, because a miracle by definition lies outside the confines of human knowledge. Or at least my knowledge, as my son figured out before very long. One day in response to "It must be a miracle," he shot back "Just

1. Weil, *Notebooks*, 243.

because you don't know the answer, Dad, doesn't mean that there isn't one!" True enough.

I teach philosophy, which has the reputation of trying to rationally explain everything and dismissively reject anything that resists such treatment. Philosophers also have the reputation of lacking humility. This reputation is, unfortunately, often well-deserved if referring to the main streams of philosophy since the scientific revolution and the Enlightenment. From its ancient roots, though, *real* philosophy begins with humility, a recognition of the ultimate inadequacy of human attempts to jam our vast, wonderful, and often terrifying reality into manageable boundaries and straitjackets.

The other ancient philosophical starting point is identified by Aristotle when he wrote that "philosophy begins with wonder." This is what a baby shows with her frank and forthright way of gazing about in bewilderment, trying to balance her oversized head on her undersized neck as she wonders "What's this thing? And what's that over there? And holy crap what's *that*?" Wonder and humility, woven together, turn philosophy, as well as theology, science, and everything else into foundational, intimately connected human activities. Psalm 8 gets this connection just right. "When I look at your heavens, the works of your fingers, the moon and the stars that you have established; what are human beings that you are mindful of them, mortals that you care for them?"[2] Wonder turns our minds and imaginations with expectation toward what transcends us, while humility continually reminds us of the vast gulf between us and what transcends us.

I heard a homily once on Jesus' feeding of the 5,000 in which the homilist struggled mightily with the very notion that so many people could be fed with five loaves and two fishes from a kid's picnic basket. After setting things up eloquently and paying proper attention to Jesus' compassion for the crowd of hungry people, the homilist hit a wall with the miracle itself. "We modern persons have a difficult time with the stories of Jesus' miracles," he said, "since what they describe violates the laws of nature." Accordingly, he did what most of us do when faced with such an apparent violation—he provided alternative interpretations of the story in which such a violation did *not* occur.

It's possible, for instance, unless Jesus was dealing with a crowd of fools that day, that the little boy was not the only person among the thousands in attendance smart enough to have brought along something to eat. The

2. Ps 8:3–4.

"miracle" is not that a tiny amount of food was increased to feed thousands, but rather that the boy's innocent generosity sparked similar generosity in others. Those who had intended to hoard their carefully packed lunches for themselves were suddenly motivated, either through inspiration or shame, to share with others around them, and instant community is formed.

And then perhaps a further "miracle" occurred, in that many realized that they didn't really need all the food they had brought—five loaves and two fishes are more than one person can eat, right? So not only does a spirit of generosity start spreading through the crowd, but gluttony takes a big hit. If everyone eats only what they need and shares the remainder, everyone has enough. An impromptu community is built on the spot, everyone learns to share with others as well as to stop eating too much, and no laws of nature are violated. Thanks be to God.

Why did the homilist, and why do all of us, find it necessary to explain a miracle away, to bring it within the confines of what we believe we know and can explain? This is partly a failure of humility, an insistence that we are the center of the universe and that, as Protagoras infamously claimed, we humans are "the measure of all things." But we're not. We are subject to the laws of nature, but these laws are neither defined by nor limited to our experience and understanding.

But our dogged attempts to explain (or explain away) everything smells more like fear than lack of humility to me. What better way to carve a home out of a reality far beyond our control than to define it in terms of what we can control? And while humility is the antidote for hubris, the cure for fear is wonder. Fear turns us inward; wonder turns us outward, toward the infinitely fascinating reality in which we find ourselves. And ultimately, wonder turns us toward God, who crosses the vast distance between the divine and human by infusing everything, including us, with transcendence.

Thomas Jefferson once published an edition of the Gospels with all the miracles taken out, resulting in a very short book. A daily existence from which miracles have been removed is similarly impoverished. A good friend of mine used to define a miracle as "something that everyone says will never, ever, ever happen and it happens anyways." And that covers just about everything, from individual acts of generosity, through impromptu human solidarity, to feeding 5,000 with a kid's lunch. As Gerard Manley Hopkins wrote, "The earth is charged with the grandeur of God."[3] We need only learn to see it with the eyes of wonder and humility.

---

3. Hopkins, *Major Works*, 128.

On its face, humility is not a popular virtue; indeed, self-effacement, being a doormat, deference to others—all popular synonyms for humility—seem more like vices than a virtue. Humility certainly doesn't fit comfortably with the dominant American notions of independence, individuality, and aggressive achievement. And yet one can scarcely read a page of the Psalms or the New Testament without encountering calls for humility. So what exactly is being called for?

Is there any of Jesus' parables more familiar than the Good Samaritan? And is there any parable whose message is more impossible to live out? The prophet Micah said that what God requires of us is "to do justice, to love mercy, and to walk humbly with your God."[4] Jesus uses the Good Samaritan story to illustrate mercy, the second of Micah's directives, agreeing with the man who concludes that the true neighbor in the story was "the one who showed mercy."[5] But it also serves as a fine gateway to the third of Micah's directives: humility.

In the Good Samaritan story, the priest, the Levite, and the Samaritan all see the man beaten, robbed, and left for dead in the ditch. And yet their manner of seeing is very different. The story says that in the case of both the priest and the Levite, "when he saw him, he passed by on the other side."[6] Chances are that both the priest and Levite assumed that the man was dead and did not want to violate the many prohibitions in the Law against those who handled holy things for a living touching anything dead. In other words, the priest and the Levite saw the injured man through the lenses of their societal roles and commitments. They saw the injured man with the eyes of the self.

"But a Samaritan while traveling came near him; and when he saw him, he was moved with pity."[7] If the Samaritan had chosen, as the priest and the Levite did, to see the injured man through self-defining lenses, he also would have walked on by. Walking on the road between Jerusalem and Jericho, the Samaritan was in enemy territory—Samaritans and Jews had nothing to do with each other. The man in the ditch was almost certainly the sort of person that the Samaritan had been taught to hate. The Samaritan is traveling, undoubtedly in a hurry, with miles to go before he

---

4. Mic 6:8.
5. Luke 10:37.
6. Luke 10:31.
7. Luke 10:35.

sleeps—why does he stop and allow his agenda to be seriously disturbed? What does he see that the priest and the Levite did not see?

The Samaritan stopped because he saw the injured man unfiltered. Simone Weil calls this ability to see in an unfiltered way "attention," and suggests that it is at the heart of true human connection. "Those who are unhappy have no need for anything in this world but people capable of giving them their attention. The capacity to give one's attention to a sufferer is a very rare and difficult thing; it is almost a miracle; it *is* a miracle."[8] Another word for this miraculous ability to see unfiltered, to attentively look at what is in front of me unencumbered by my usual filters and agendas, is *humility*. And it is at the heart of true faith.

This is why defining ourselves morally in terms of positions taken on hot button issues is far more attractive than actually attempting to live a life guided by what the texts and principles of one's faith actually demand. Human beings are not naturally wired in this way. Our natural state is to consider ourselves as the center of everything, to overestimate our power and importance, and to behave as if we are the only thing in the universe that matters. The Good Samaritan is miraculous because he is able to truly see what is front of him and respond directly without a moment's concern for anything other than what this man needs.

If Iris Murdoch is right when defining love as the recognition that something other than oneself is real, then love and humility go hand in hand. Love and humility energize the apprehension of something else, something particular, as existing outside us. In our daily lives we are continually confronting something other than ourselves. We all not only can but have to deal with the resistant otherness of other persons, other things, history, the natural world, and this involves perpetual effort. But at the heart of the Christian faith, illustrated by the parable of the Good Samaritan, is the promise that the possibility of transformative love and humility is in each of us, ready to be introduced into the world if we will only look away from ourselves toward what is directly in front of us.

We are called to cultivate Good Samaritan moments—moments in which the human being in front of us is not dark-skinned, poor, female, gay, conservative, wealthy, Muslim, male, straight, ugly, liberal, old, Christian, obese, or attractive, but rather is a person whose needs, hopes and dreams are real and independent of us. It takes effort to come to see the world as it is, a task that can only be attempted with the miraculous energy

---

8. Weil, *Waiting*, 64.

of humility. When I believe that I have seen all there is to see, the Christ in me says "let me look again."

In the early hours of one Sunday morning, I read the final pages of Daša Drndić's *Trieste*, the most powerfully unrelenting and unforgiving book related to the Holocaust I have ever read. On the back cover, a reviewer wrote, "*Trieste* is not a book for the faint-hearted, either in style or subject.... Enter if you are brave enough, and if you stay the course you will be changed." No one—those in authority, the church, those who turned their heads, those who simply did whatever they could to stay alive—is spared in this brutally honest and unflinching account of what human beings are capable of.

As I read I was reminded of something post-Holocaust Jewish theologian Irving Greenberg said: "No statement, theological or otherwise, should be made that could not be made with credibility in the presence of the burning children."[9] With regard to those men who were at the same time both murderous killers and yet tender fathers and husbands, Drndić argues that a father is not "a sacrosanct being.... There are no sacrosanct beings. Even God is not sacrosanct, perhaps He least of all."[10] To those who wish to excuse the culpable silence and frequent collaboration of religious institutions, she writes that "this caricatured parade and more than revolting fabrication, this costumed theatre of transparent lies and empty promises should be done away with right now, once and for all."[11]

And then Jeanne and I went to church. I was lector, she was chalice bearer—we couldn't skip, but I was hardly in the mood. I was responsible for the first reading of the morning from Isaiah, a text I had briefly glanced at during the week, describing it to Jeanne as "kind of weird." At the lectern, I found myself giving voice to something unexpectedly disturbing.

Isaiah 58 begins with the prophet mimicking the complaints of the "house of Jacob": we have been fasting and humbling ourselves, just as you require. Why aren't you answering our prayers? Why aren't you taking notice? In response the prophet laughs with the voice of God. "Look, you serve your own interest on your fast day, and oppress all your workers. Look, you fast only to quarrel and to fight. Is such the fast that I choose?... Is it to

---

9. Quoted in Williamson, *A Guest*, 13.
10. Drndić, *Trieste*, 342.
11. Ibid., 343.

bow down the head like a bulrush, and to lie in sackcloth and ashes?"[12] In other words, your "fast day" is all about you. It's all about your pitiful and self-centered attempts to twist divine favor in your direction. It's all about having convinced yourself that skipping a few meals, attending a few extra meetings at your preferred house of worship, and arguing with each other about which forms of ritual are best, are all that it takes to draw God's favorable attention. "You call this a fast, a day acceptable to the Lord?"[13]

You want to know what a *real* fast day would be like? What it would *really* be like if you humbled yourselves? Here's a clue:

> To loose the bonds of injustice
> To undo the thongs of the yoke
> To let the oppressed go free
> To share your bread with the hungry
> To bring the homeless and poor into your house
> To cover the naked when you see them.[14]

Try doing *that* for a while and see what happens.

Jesus says this sort of thing frequently in the Gospels. But in Isaiah's prophetic tones, the call to attend to the hungry, poor, widows, and orphans is not a suggestion or an invitation to try out something new, as we might mistakenly read the New Testament texts. The text from Isaiah is a flat-out command. Just f--king do it. And until you do, stop pretending that you are anything other than a self-centered piece of garbage. And stop expecting anything other than a perpetuation of the continuing, sad human story of injustice and violence. Period.

When one of the characters in Albert Camus's *The Plague* is described as a "saint," he responds "Sanctity doesn't really appeal to me.... What interests me is being a man."[15] This strikes me as a good place to start. A central problem illuminated by texts such as *Trieste* and Isaiah is the powerful human tendency to set the moral bar so low that even the most basic moral behavior looks like heroism or sainthood. We are told in sacred texts over and over again that God demands that we be fundamentally aware of each other, but this exceeds our minimalist moral expectations of ourselves. In truth, the belief that basic morality and common decency require a con-

---

12. Isa 58:3, 5.
13. Isa 58:5.
14. Isa 58:6–7.
15. Camus, *The Plague*, 255.

scious awareness of needs other than our own, particularly those of other human beings, need not be rooted in religious faith or practice. Whatever it takes to convince even a few of us that not only our thriving, but our very existence and survival depends on expanding the membership of our moral community to more than one is worth hanging on to.

On the final page of *The Plague*, at the end of a harrowing tale of individuals fighting against an out-of-control evil that could not be stopped, the main character, Dr. Rieux, takes stock of what he has learned now that the plague has left as inexplicably as it came.

> He knew that the tale he had to tell could not be one of a final victory. It could be only the record of what had had to be done, and what assuredly would have to be done again in the never ending fight against terror and its relentless onslaughts, despite their personal afflictions, by all who, while unable to be a saint but refusing to bow down to pestilences, strive their utmost to be healers.[16]

I recently read an article in *Harper's* online magazine by physicist and novelist Alan Lightman entitled "Our Place in the Universe." The point of the essay is to put us in our place, so to speak. For instance, the most distant galaxy scientist have yet seen is about 100,000,000,000,000,000,000,000 miles away from earth—"give or take."[17] Contemporary scientists "have revealed a world as far removed from us as colors are from the blind."[18]

It might make sense, then to focus our attention on "this island home" where we seem to have a certain amount of central importance. Not so fast—"the totality of living matter on Earth—humans and animals, plants, bacteria, and pond scum—makes up 0.00000001 percent of the mass of the planet."[19] Combine that figure with the current estimate that only three percent of all the stars in the universe are accompanied by a potentially life-sustaining planet, then in the unlikely event that all of those planets actually do have life, then we can estimate that the fraction of stuff in the visible universe that exists in living form is something like 0.000000000000001 percent, or one millionth of one billionth of 1 percent.

> If some cosmic intelligence created the universe, life would seem to have been only an afterthought. And if life emerges by random

---

16. Ibid., 308.
17. Lightman, "Our Place," line 30.
18. Ibid., lines 165–66.
19. Ibid., lines 174–75.

Humility—From Infinity to Intimacy

> processes, vast amounts of lifeless material are needed for each particle of life. Such numbers cannot help but bear upon the question of our significance in the universe.[20]

Such sobering numbers and observations, of course, are nothing new. The great seventeenth-century French mathematician, scientist, and religious philosopher Blaise Pascal has a memorable meditation on apparent human insignificance in his *Pensées*.

> Let man then contemplate the whole of nature in its lofty and full majesty . . . . This whole visible world is only an imperceptible trace in the amplitude of nature. . . . Let man consider what he is . . . as lost in this remote corner of nature, and from the little cell in which he finds himself lodged, I mean the universe, let him learn to estimate the just value of the earth, kingdoms, cities, and himself.[21]

After several paragraphs of his own version of putting us in our place, Pascal concludes with this haunting one-liner: *The eternal silence of these infinite spaces frightens me.*[22]

Reminders that we are not special, more importantly that I am not special, are always needed regardless of whether they are welcomed. Yet what most struck me in the "Our Place in the Universe" piece occurs right at the beginning when Lightman introduces us to the astronomer who is investigating the galaxy that is 100,000,000,000,000,000,000,000 miles away from earth.

> The prize for exploring the greatest distance in space goes to a man named Garth Illingworth, who works in a ten-by-fifteen-foot office at the University of California, Santa Cruz. Illingworth studies galaxies so distant that their light has traveled through space for more than 13 billion years to get here. His office is packed with tables and chairs, bookshelves, computers, scattered papers, issues of *Nature*, and a small refrigerator and a microwave to fuel research that can extend into the wee hours of the morning.[23]

Within the confines of an office not much larger than a medieval monk's cell, a human being is analyzing an image created by light that has been

---

20. Ibid., lines 177–78.
21. Pascal, *Penseés*, 58.
22. Ibid., 64.
23. Lightman, "Our Place," lines 17–22.

traveling for three times as long as the best estimated age of the Earth. Pascal reminds us to "consider our condition: we are something, and we are not everything."[24]

> Man is only a reed, the weakest thing in nature, but he is a thinking reed. The whole universe does not need to take up arms to crush him; a vapor, a drop of water, is enough to kill him. But if the universe were to crush him, man would still be nobler than what kills him, because he knows he is dying and the advantage the universe has over him. The universe knows nothing of this. All our dignity consists, then, in thought.... Let us labor to think well.[25]

Lightman's essay brings us face to face with the infinite, not just the infinite physical spaces that Pascal is frightened of but, for those of us who are God-obsessed, this also leads directly to the divine. For we do not seek to establish a toe-hold on infinity just when we turn our attention away from ourselves toward the vast physical universe. We are also participating in the same sort of activity as Garth Illingworth when we seek to "think clearly" about what is greater than us—the divine, God, the infinite, the One, whatever you choose to call it. Often this is best done by analogy and by telling stories. In *Philosophical Fragments*, Soren Kierkegaard tells a lovely story about a powerful king who falls in love with a lowly maiden. The maiden is unaware of the king's love, and the king is worried. Knowing that love is built on equality, how is the gap between his royal greatness and her humble maidenhood to be crossed? He does not want to coerce her into loving him by revealing his love in all his splendor, nor would elevating her to royal status work, since then she would simply be the same lowly maiden with a better wardrobe and job description.

The only possible solution to the king's problem is remarkably simple. "Since union could not be brought about by an elevation it must be attempted by a descent."[26] The king must step down from his royal throne and enter the maiden's hut as an equal. Not as a king in a peasant's costume, but as a peasant. Only then can he be sure that she might return his love because of the person he is rather than because of the role he inhabits. The king's advisors and courtiers are astounded—how to explain the choice to leave royalty behind for a simple girl? And this, Kierkegaard reminds us, is precisely the mystery and madness of love, not only of the king for

---

24. Pascal, *Penseés*, 61.
25. Ibid., 64.
26. Kierkegaard, *Fragments*, 39.

the maiden, but also of God for human beings. "This is the unfathomable nature of love, that it desires equality with the beloved, not in jest merely, but in earnest and truth."[27]

Across the infinite gap separating the human and the divine, God comes to us by becoming one of us. What a remarkable response to our fear of "the eternal silence of the infinite spaces." God is not silent—God's love turns infinity into intimacy. If I embrace this story, what must my response be in return? As Kierkegaard reminds us, this requires nothing less than my willingness for everything to change.

> When the seed of the oak is planted in earthen vessels, they break asunder; when new wine is poured in old leathern bottles, they burst; what must happen when God implants himself in human weakness unless man becomes a new vessel and a new creature![28]

---

27. Ibid.
28. Ibid., 42–43.

11

Beauty—Where the Divine and the Human Meet

As Jeanne headed into Dunkin' Donuts to purchase her customary large decaf French Vanilla with eight creams and three Equals (and pity the fool who doesn't get it right), I stayed in the car surfing the FM dial—my coffee intake for the morning had already exceeded its quota. I landed on New York's NPR classical station just in time to hear "Ombra mai fu," the opening aria from Georg Friedrich Handel's 1738 opera, *Serse*. If you are not familiar with this aria, stop reading right now, YouTube it, and spend the next three and a half minutes in heaven (I recommend the Kathleen Battle version). Parked in an ugly Double-D parking lot on Long Island, I thought to myself that when the angels sing, they must begin and close with this piece—perhaps the most beautiful I've ever heard.

    A couple of weeks earlier while writing an essay on our backyard deck, I heard the distinctive call of a cardinal, my favorite bird—other than penguins, who don't show up in Rhode Island very often. As I paused to listen, the cardinal flew in all of his scarlet glory to perch on the branch of a dead tree in our neighbor's yard, about fifteen feet from where I was sitting. I thought for a moment about quietly switching my tablet to camera mode and trying to get a picture, but chose instead to simply be with my feathered friend. "Hey, dude," I said—"looking good!" He sang his distinctive song for me a couple more times, then darted off on his cardinal way.

Beauty—Where the Divine and the Human Meet

Moments of beauty such as these, even if only a few minutes long, go far toward sustaining my deep belief in the goodness of things, despite what appears to be daily and overwhelming evidence to the contrary. Such moments, Joan Chittister writes, "are the heartbeat of the universe. They make us glad to be alive."[1]

The sea pronounces something, over and over, in a hoarse whisper. I cannot quite make it out.[2] —Annie Dillard

I live in the Ocean State, but I really don't like the ocean very much. I am well aware that many people are ocean worshipers and can't think of anything more attractive, peaceful, and fulfilling than a day either at an ocean beach or on a boat on the water. I'm not part of your club. Some look at or experience the ocean and are struck by feelings of peace and beauty. The ocean is indeed beautiful, but for me its beauty speaks of power, vastness, and a certain amount of fear. During the week a few summers ago on retreat that I woke up every morning with the Big Sur Pacific at my feet, I always felt a bit tense and edgy, as if I was in danger of being swallowed up. The beauty of the ocean puts some people in a peaceful place, but it makes me nervous. Simone Weil once observed that the flowing, ever-changing folds of ocean waves are no less beautiful because we know that sometimes they wreck ships and drown people. "On the contrary," she writes, "this adds to the ocean's beauty."[3]

Immanuel Kant had this tension in mind when he distinguished in his philosophy between the "Beautiful" and the "Sublime." The Beautiful refers to things that are, well, beautiful—in the sense that they produce aesthetic pleasure and feelings of happiness. Things that are Sublime can also be beautiful, but tend to overwhelm us, disturb us, or even frighten us. The Sublime is "awesome" and "terrible" in the original senses of the words—it inspires awe and terror. Are you attracted and repelled by the same thing or experience? Do you consider something to be both beautiful and terrifying in its awesome, often destructive power? That's the Sublime—and that's what the ocean causes in me. It is both beautiful and disturbing, attractive and frightening. The ocean is sublime.

1. Chittister, *Essential Writings*, 119.
2. Dillard, *Teaching a Stone*, 65.
3. Weil, *Simone Weil*, 50.

The authors of the Psalms in the Jewish scriptures have a strong sense of this. Over and over again, the psalmist reminds us of the awesome power and terror of the sea; even more provocatively, these reflections are frequently used as a bridge to talking about God, the ultimate example of sublimity. Sometimes the psalmist describes the power of the sea, assuring us that God's power is even greater. Psalm 33 tells us, for instance, that "God collects the waves of the ocean; and collects the waves of the sea,"[4] in control of even the most terrifying force imaginable. This can be source of comfort:

> God is for us a refuge and strength, a helper close at hand in time of distress, so we shall not fear though the earth should rock, though the mountains fall into the depths of the sea, even though its waters rage and foam, even though the mountains be shaken by its waves.[5]

Sometimes the psalmist cries out for rescue from the often ocean-like overwhelming power of human reality:

> Save me from the waters of the deep lest the waves overwhelm me. Do not let the deep engulf me, nor death close its mouth on me.[6]

At other times, the sublime, fearsome aspects of the ocean are attributed directly to God.

> Deep is calling upon deep, in the roar of waters; your torrents and all your waves swept over me.[7]

It is one thing to seek divine protection from the terrible and awful contingencies of human experience; it is another to attribute that very terrible and awful beauty to the divine itself. If what is greater than me is the epitome of the sublime, meaning that it not only is inexpressibly beautiful but also is unpredictable and terrifying, how do I respond? Is it possible for a mere, non-sublime human being to be in relationship with something like that?

If I am disturbed and made nervous by the ocean, there is a simple solution—stay away from the ocean. Good advice, but for me at least similar advice does not work concerning God. No matter how unpredictable and disturbing the divine might be, I can't turn away. That being the case, I find

---

4. Ps 33:7.
5. Ps 46:1–4.
6. Ps 69:2–3.
7. Ps 42:8.

the following simple observation from Rowan Williams helpful: "If you want to swim, you must begin to understand the sea."[8] The Jewish mystics go so far as to suggest that if God is like the ocean, we are the waves on that ocean. That's a bit esoteric for my taste, but the point is clear—God invites an intimacy so close that at times the horizon between the divine and human becomes as blurry as the horizon between the ocean and sky at Big Sur. And isn't that the promise of incarnation—the fusion of divinity and humanity? The older I get and the more time I spend struggling with divine sublimity, the more I am convinced that this is not a problem to be solved or an issue to be sorted out. It is rather something to be lived. I agree with the author of Psalm 84—"My soul longs and thirsts for the living God."[9]

Rather than a problem to be solved, the world is a joyful mystery to be contemplated with gladness and praise.[10] —Pope Francis

Great artists tell us that predictability, regularity and order are deadly to beauty of any sort, natural or otherwise. Pierre-Auguste Renoir once said that

> Beauty of every description finds its charm in variety. Nature abhors both vacuum and regularity. For the same reason, no work of art can really be called such if it has not been created by an artist who believes in irregularity and rejects any set form. Regularity, order, desire for perfection (which is always a false perfection) destroy art. The only possibility of maintaining taste in art is to impress on artists and the public the importance of irregularity. Irregularity is the basis of all art.[11]

And Charles Baudelaire observed that

> That which is not slightly distorted lacks sensible appeal; from which it follows that irregularity—that is to say, the unexpected, surprise and astonishment, are an essential part and characteristic of beauty.[12]

---

8. Chittister and Williams, *Uncommon Gratitude*, 141.
9. Ps 84:3.
10. Pope Francis, *Laudato Si'*, 13.
11. Eisenstein, *Film Form*, 51.
12. Ibid.

Irregularity, the unexpected, novelty, even the disturbing and edgy not only contribute to what is beautiful—they arguably define it.

This throws various interesting doors wide open. Why, for instance, are human beings tuned to beauty on frequencies and wavelengths that intersect with the seeming contradictories of beauty? Once again we find that traditional binaries such as sacred vs. profane, good vs. evil, right vs. wrong, individual vs. community, and so on are not opposites at all. Such binaries are so intimately and intricately interwoven that only a forced, surface-level interpretation can insist on their absolute independence of each other. Annie Dillard, one of her generation's most interesting and creative observers of the natural world, writes that she went to live for several months by a creek in the wilderness "to see what I could see." And what Dillard sees is that "Terror and a beauty insoluble are a ribbon of blue woven into the fringes of garments of things both great and small."[13] From the slow-train-wreck horror of watching a giant water bug paralyze a small frog then suck the frog's insides out through a puncture hole to the gratuitous beauty of a mockingbird free-falling from a five-story roof only to swerve and land light as a feather just a couple of feet before crashing into the earth—just because it can—Dillard finds that we are surrounded by endless details that belie our constant attempts to categorize and "figure out." Is this objectively true of the world we find ourselves in, or is this a fascinating feature of human observers? Is the world really this way or are we, products of the evolutionary process, wired to experience the world in this way? Both? Neither?

I am fascinated with the question of what this complex mixture of good and evil, beauty and violence, regularity and irregularity, the predictable and the novel, might tell us about the creative force that put all of this into being and motion. Perhaps nothing. Perhaps all of the above is best explained naturalistically with no reference to anything greater than us. But on the assumption that there is something greater than us that has something to do with the reality in which we find ourselves, what might be said? What could God have been thinking in fashioning such a world? Whatever else might be said, this definitely ain't your parents' God. This is not the traditional clockmaker God who created, then continues to tinker with, and fine-tune, a cosmic machine.

If our world was designed with precision, order, and economy in mind, the designer was having a pretty bad day. Darwin opened the door wide to speculation that the world we live in is vastly more messy and open-ended

---

13. Dillard, *Pilgrim*, 27.

than we ever imagined; a century and a half of further investigation in all of the various sciences has confirmed Darwin's insight. It's very possible to investigate the messy, inefficient, and spectacularly fascinating universe we inhabit without reference to anything greater than ourselves, but I find it impossible to do so. If we are in fact part of a creation that is unfinished, a universe that in Teilhard de Chardin's memorable phrase "God does not make: He makes things make themselves,"[14] where does intelligent speculation about such a creator lead? In directions both stimulating and iconoclastic.

Two of the traditional characteristics attributed to God, for instance, are omniscience and omnipotence. God knows everything and has the power to do anything. Such "omni" characteristics have been problematic for centuries when thinking about human choice and freedom. When thinking about an open-ended universe that continues to be created by the creatures that inhabit it, such characteristics are more than problematic—they need to be jettisoned entirely, as many cutting-edge scientists and theologians suggest. In an interview with Krista Tippett, physicist John Polkinghorne suggests a new way of thinking about this:

> The act of creation, the act of bringing into being a world in which creatures are allowed to be themselves, to make themselves, is an act of love. It is an act of divine self-limitation. The theologians like to call it *kenosis* from the Greek word. God is not the puppet master of the universe, pulling every string. God has taken, if you like, a risk. Creation is more like an improvisation than the performance of a fixed score that God wrote in eternity. And that sort of world involves God accepting limitations, and, I believe, accepting limitations such as not knowing the future.[15]

A God who is more like Ella Fitzgerald than Beethoven—now *that's* interesting.

Rather than a tightly controlled and designed universe, this is a universe in which power and knowledge on the part of the divine are sacrificed for—something. Freedom? Choice? Beauty? At the very least, the motivations for such an ongoing creative process are something other than control and order. A world in which creatures are empowered to create in novel and unique ways sounds less like a universe energized by ordering power and more like one embedded with creative love and emerging beauty, a beauty

---

14. Teilhard de Chardin, *Christianity*, 28.
15. Tippett, *Einstein's God*, 269.

that theologian John Haught defines as "ordered novelty."[16] Only a universe structured on the edge of order and chaos could generate such results.

The soul's natural inclination to love beauty is the trap God most frequently uses in order to win it and open it to the breath from on high.[17] —Simone Weil

Speculations about what the beauty and disorder of the natural world might tell us about the divine were at the heart of a seminar with honors students entitled "Beauty and Violence" that I taught recently, to both the delight and dismay of my students, a delight and dismay often occurring in the same person. For some of my students, the implications were fascinating and liberating, while for others they were disturbing and paradigm-shifting. As one of my students said during her oral final examination, "This class really messed me up—in a good way." A God who intentionally created a partially finished, non-economical, and messy universe that is still a project in the making is not a God who knows everything that will happen or inserts divine power into every organizational detail. This is a God who has taken a significant risk—on us. In an intellectual notebook entry, one of my students captured this idea concisely and beautifully.

> God is only truly taking a risk if He has a desired intention for us—a purpose, so to speak—that could either be fulfilled or unfulfilled through our free actions and the way in which we live our lives. God is gambling on us because He has allowed for the opportunity of failure. God has fixed His hand by giving us everything we need to fulfill our purpose. He is actually no less omnipotent, he is simply using His power to limit His power, a theory that if true would be the noblest of all divine endeavors. If we deny our egos, we are to be awakened by His silence and transformed by the realization of our limitations.

This, of course, raises many more questions than it answers. But they are better questions in my estimation than the traditional ones, in keeping with my favored definition of philosophy as "the art of asking better and better questions." Yet another confirmation that Socrates was right when he said that "the unexamined life is not worth living."

16. Haught, *God*, 139.
17. Weil, *Waiting*, 103.

Beauty—Where the Divine and the Human Meet

An adjusted and retooled observation of the beauty of the world is an important component of beginning to understand just what the divine presence behind it all might be up to. Simone Weil saw intimations of the incarnation in the beauty of the world, writing that "the longing to love the beauty of the world in a human being is essentially the longing for the Incarnation."[18] Our powerful human attraction to beauty is the "trap" the divine uses to turn our attention toward things greater than ourselves. In the beauty of the world we encounter a marker not only of transcendence, but also of the possibility of contact between the transcendent and the human.

> God created the universe, and his Son, our first-born brother, created the beauty of it for us. The beauty of the world is Christ's tender smile for us coming through matter. He is really present in the universal beauty. The love of this beauty proceeds from God dwelling in our souls and goes out to God present in the universe. It also is like a sacrament.[19]

The beauty of the world is both sacramental and incarnational, a literal instance of the divine inhabiting matter, a pointer toward what is greater than ourselves.

Seeing the beauty of the world as incarnational and sacramental leads directly to concern and care for a natural world that is endangered by human neglect and abuse. In the introduction to his remarkable encyclical *Laudato Si'*, Pope Francis quotes Ecumenical Patriarch Bartholomew, the spiritual leader of the world's 300 million Orthodox Christians, as follows:

> To commit a crime against the natural world is a sin against ourselves and sin against God. . . . As Christians we are also called to accept the world as a sacrament of communion, as a way of sharing with God and our neighbors on a global scale. It is our humble conviction that the divine and the human meet in the slightest detail in the seamless garment of God's creation, in the last speck of dust of our planet.[20]

Care for the earth, cultivation of our intimate connectedness with everything, and above all a recognition of the sacredness of everything are proper responses to beauty. The fact that we inhabit a world that appears to

---

18. Ibid., 104.
19. Ibid.
20. Pope Francis, *Laudato Si'*, 10–11.

be reflective of an exuberant and endlessly innovative artist rather than the precise and logical result of a rational inventor raises the stakes immeasurably concerning what is required of us. As Pope Francis writes,

> The universe did not emerge as the result of arbitrary omnipotence, a show of force or a desire for self-assertion. Creation is of the order of love. . . . Creating a world in need of development, God in some way sought to limit himself in such a way that many of the things we think of as evils, dangers or sources of suffering, are in reality part of the pains of childbirth which he uses to draw us into the act of cooperation with the Creator.[21]

As is my frequent custom, I shared my unexpected and much appreciated encounter with Handel's "Ombra mai fu" that I described at the beginning of this chapter with my Facebook acquaintances, then a day later on my blog. Several who share my love of classical music shared their own favorite versions of the aria on YouTube; a good-natured debate arose over whether the aria is most beautiful in the soprano range, as Handel wrote it, or transposed into the lower and richer mezzo-soprano or contralto ranges. The music is so glorious that I, not knowing Italian, speculated that the text of the aria was probably religiously themed along the lines of so many of Handel's compositions. But no—the text of "Ombra mai fu" contains no lofty sentiments, no paeans to the divine. It's a brief poem of thanks for the shade of a plane tree.

> Never was a shade
> of any plant
> dearer and more lovely,
> or more sweet.

Over the centuries Handel's beautiful tune has been co-opted for different texts, such as the hymn "Holy Art Thou." But it is fitting that one of the most inspired pieces of music ever written is originally in honor of a tree. One of the greatest continuing insights of John Ames, the aging Calvinist minister from Marilynne Robinson's *Gilead*, concerns the sacredness of all things. As he nears the end of his life, he pays close attention to the mystery and miracle of things most of us dismiss as "ordinary."

> It has seemed to me sometimes as though the Lord breathes on this poor gray ember of Creation and it turns to radiance—for a

---

21. Ibid., 60.

moment or a year or the span of a life. And then it sinks back into itself again, and to look at it no one would know it had anything to do with fire, or light. . . . Wherever you turn your eyes the world can shine like transfiguration. You don't have to bring a thing to it except a little willingness to see. Only, who has the courage to see it?[22]

For Ames, everything is a sacrament with intimations of holiness. And the divine being he has served and conversed with for decades is still a mystery.

"You don't have to bring a thing to it except a little willingness to see. Only, who has the courage to see it?" Good question. It takes a lot more courage to embrace this world with all of its imperfections and disappointments as a spectacular and continuing divine miracle than to step back and bemoan the fact that it seldom is the miracle *we* would have performed if it were up to us. It isn't up to us—the power and glory of our created, sacred world is far above our pay scale. And yet sacredness and beauty embedded in imperfect matter is a reminder that according to the Christian narrative, this very strange yet compelling fusion of the divine and the imperfect is God's intention with us.

---

22. Robinson, *Gilead*, 245.

12

Hope—I Will Bring You Home

Along with millions of others worldwide, Jeanne and I are huge fans of the television phenomenon *Downton Abbey*. Late last year Jeanne signed up to throw a few monthly dollars in the direction of our local PBS station; in return, we were shipped the full fifth season of the series on DVD at the end of January. The fifth season had just started its Sunday evening Masterpiece Theater run a couple of weeks earlier here in the States, and now we had in our hands the rest of the season with no need to ration the episodes out one week at a time. The DVDs showed up a couple of days before we got smacked with Winter Storm Juno, the first and worst of a series of winter storms that came in unrelenting succession over the next couple of months. With Tuesday and then Wednesday classes cancelled and the good fortune of not losing our electricity, we binge-watched Lord Grantham along with his relatives and homies cavort and angst through eight straight episodes—about eleven or twelve hours of viewing. And we wanted more.

All Downton fans have their favorite characters—Mr. Carson, the erstwhile butler of the establishment, is mine. But *everyone* loves Lord Grantham's mother Violet, the dowager countess and source of endless entertainment from meaningful glances to pithy retorts, a lovably manipulative force behind virtually everything going on in each episode with a wit as dry as a martini. In this season any number of Violet one-liners made me laugh, then think. Violet is the perpetual pragmatist, and this comment to her granddaughter Mary particularly caught my attention. *Hope is a tease to prevent us from accepting reality.*

Hope—I Will Bring You Home

To which the idealist responds that realism or pragmatism is a device to help us avoid dreaming of and hoping for what could be rather than settling for what is. I like to think of myself as a "pragmatic idealist" or perhaps an "optimistic realist." These things really are not contradictory, although many (including Violet) assume that they are. The philosopher in me tends toward realism, with Aristotle, David Hume, and William James as three of my most important philosophical influences—realists and pragmatists all. Yet that realism is tempered by my faith, which both applies directly to the real world I struggle with every day and offers transcendent hope that there is more to reality than what I struggle with every day. Balancing pragmatism and hope is central to my project of managing to be both a philosopher and a Christian, something that a good friend many years ago worried that I would not be able to pull off.

Cyprian Consiglio, the Benedictine monk, theologian, hermitage prior and musician who ran the retreat I attended in Minnesota not long ago defines *liturgy* as "ideology in action." Annie Dillard defines it as "certain words which people have successfully addressed to God without their getting killed."[1] I like both of these definitions. I have a deep resonance with liturgy, especially liturgy expressed in music, something surprising given that there was no liturgy in my Baptist world growing up. Although "ideology" is usually something I accuse people I disagree with of embracing, Cyprian's definition reminds me that at its core, ideology is simply the collection of beliefs, stories, ideas, and commitments, some conscious and some unconscious, that guides a person's actions and frames a person's life. We are all ideologues. Liturgical frameworks provide containers that shape this collection with reference to what is greater than us. Annie's definition is a reminder that the very attempt to say or do anything with content and meaning referring to what is greater than us is at best misguided, at worst ridiculous.

Of the many varieties of liturgical celebration I have encountered over the past few years, the most striking is the Good Friday morning prayer service I have experienced twice with the Benedictine monks at St. John's Abbey in Minnesota. The tone for the day is set as a solitary monk chants the entire book of Lamentations from the Jewish scriptures. Lamentations is undoubtedly the most depressing book in the Bible, perhaps anywhere, a

---

1. Dillard, *Holy*, 59.

litany of five poetic dirges over the destruction of Jerusalem. Traditionally attributed to the prophet Jeremiah, the tone of the poems is bleak: God does not speak, the degree of suffering is described as undeserved, and expectations of future redemption are minimal. In Psalm 129 the psalmist writes "The plowers plowed on my back; they made their furrows long"[2]—Lamentations is page after page of that sentiment.

I was reminded of this Good Friday liturgy as I entered our campus chapel for a memorial service honoring a friend and colleague who had tragically died far too soon in an automobile accident. As I settled into my seat with the several hundred persons who closed offices and canceled classes in the middle of the day to honor and celebrate her life, I noticed in the program that the reading from the Jewish scriptures was from Lamentations. "That's appropriate," I thought. "At least there's nothing in Lamentations that will give us the unwelcome advice that we should not feel the devastating loss and sadness that we feel." But I had forgotten that roughly halfway through the poems, Jeremiah comes up briefly for air.

> But this I call to mind, and therefore I have hope:
> The steadfast love of the Lord never ceases, his mercies never come to an end;
> They are new every morning; great is your faithfulness.
> "The Lord is my portion," says my soul, "therefore I will hope in him."
> The Lord is good to those who wait for him, to the soul that seeks him.
> It is good that one should wait quietly for the salvation of the Lord.[3]

A few years ago a dynamic, fresh new face burst onto the American political scene promising "Hope and Change"; not long afterwards Sarah Palin, not particularly enamored of this new guy, snarkily asked "How's that hopey changey thing working out for ya?" Politics aside, it's a good question. The Apostle Paul famously wrote, "Now faith, hope, and love abide, these three; and the greatest of these is love."[4] But he forgot to add that the most challenging of these is hope. Hope is a tough nut to crack—of the big three at the end of the passage in 1 Corinthians, love and faith, as challenging as they are, strike me as easier to get a handle on than hope.

Advent is the liturgical season of hope—my favorite of all the liturgical seasons because it means that the semester is almost over, I like purple,

---

2. Psa 129:3.
3. Lam 3:21–26.
4. 1 Cor 13:13.

enjoy the Advent carols that only come around once a year, appreciate the opportunity to do something other than slog through the interminable Ordinary Time that stretches from Pentecost to the Sunday after Thanksgiving, and because I am by nature a very hopeful person. But it has been a bit of a tough sell for me lately, with seemingly daily evidence that the world is a mess, no one has the capacity or wants to do anything about it, accompanied by tragic reminders that human life is fleeting and even the best can be taken away in a moment. "The world really sucks," Jeanne commented as we listened to NPR one morning on the way downtown to the bus station so she could visit her sister whose husband just died. And it does suck. But if we are willing to poke our heads up even momentarily from the crap, Lamentations tells us that hope is always available—and is a choice.

Providence College's annual Advent Lessons and Carols Service always opens with a beautiful Advent hymn:

> O come, divine Messiah!
> The world in silence waits the day
> When hope shall sing its triumph,
> And sadness flee away.

Who doesn't want sadness to flee away? But when the sadness is palpable, when the night is especially dark, what hope can a song offer? More importantly, do we have any reason to believe that what we hope for—a divine presence in the midst of human sadness and darkness—is anything more than a nice story we repeat regularly in order to convince ourselves that there is a glimmer of meaning in a horribly dark world?

According to Lamentations, we have reason to hope if we choose to have it. And the reason to hope will not be found in external events, which will be as they will be. Hope finds its home in waiting, in silence, in emptiness, and in the conviction that there is more going on than meets the eye. There are as many ways to nurture the space of quietness and silence within as there are people containing that space. Our task is to be ready, to prepare a space for hope and promise to be nurtured, even when every external indicator is that hopelessness and despair are the order of the day.

For an academic department seeking to hire a new faculty colleague for the following academic year, January and February are busy months. These are the months during which finalists are chosen, interviews are conducted, and job offers are made. I have been a search committee member

Freelance Christianity

seven or eight times, chairing the committee four of those times. As I reviewed the various dossiers during a recent search, something jumped out at me in a semifinalist's written response to the college mission statement (required of all semifinalists) that I had either missed or ignored the first time through. The candidate wrote that "A dear friend and colleague with whom I shared an office for many years once confided in me that he could hardly believe that I was really religious, for I seemed like such a reasonable man. Religion is good for children," the candidate's office mate continued, "but in adults, belief in God is a sign of psychological disorder."

In keeping with the often haphazard workings of my brain, I was immediately reminded of an episode from the first season of HBO's series *True Detective*. Marty Hart and Rust Cohle are detective partners, but could not be more different. Hart has a well-developed "good ole boy" persona that masks a number of personal quirks and demons that are slowly revealed over the weekly episodes, while Cohle wears his intelligence, pessimism, and misanthropy on his sleeve. Their pursuit of a serial and ritualistic killer brings them to a tent revival meeting, where from the back they observe and discuss a gathering of a hundred or so believers held in rapt attention by the preacher at the front.

Rust: What do you think the average IQ of this group is?

Marty: Can you see Texas up there on your high horse? What do you know about these people?

Rust: Just observation and deduction. I see a propensity for obesity, poverty, a yen for fairy tales. Folks putting what bucks they do have into a wicker basket being passed around. Safe to say nobody here's going to be splitting the atom, Marty.

Marty: See that? Your f--kin' attitude. Not everybody wants to sit around in an empty room and get off on murder manuals. Some folks enjoy community, the common good.

Rust: If the common good's got to make up fairy tales, it's not good for anybody.

Marty: Can you imagine if people *didn't* believe, the things they would get up to?

Rust: The same things they do now, just out in the open.

Marty: Bullshit. It would be a f--king freak show of murder and debauchery, and you know it.

Rust: If the only thing keeping a person decent is the expectation of divine reward, then brother that person is a piece of shit. And I'd like to get as many of them out in the open as possible.

Marty: I guess your judgment is infallible, piece of shit wise. Do you think your notebook is a stone tablet?

Rust: What's it say about a life that you got to get together, tell yourself stories that violate every law of the universe just to get through the goddamn day? What's that say about your reality, Marty?

Marty: I don't use ten-dollar words as much as you, but for someone who sees no point in existence, you sure fret about it an awful lot. And you still sound panicked.

Is religious belief an "opiate of the masses," a haven for shallow-thinking individuals who seek comfort, community, and an escape from their lousy lives, or perhaps the most dependable firewall against life in a state of nature that would, as Thomas Hobbes put it, be "solitary, poor, nasty, brutish, and short"?[5] Or is it something else altogether? The job applicant's office mate and Rust Cohle both assume that common sense and clear thinking rule out what is presumed to be at the heart of all religious belief—the sort of magical and wishful thinking that one is supposed to grow out of as one matures. Magical thinking does an end run on the hard work of grappling with how things actually are, replacing such work with wishful thinking and unsubstantiated hopes.

But calling everything that cannot be reduced to empirical facts "magical thinking" is prematurely dismissive. Is there no place for hope in the life of a thinking, rational person? Is it never legitimate to hope for and believe in something that cannot be fully substantiated with a combination of past experience and present available facts and data? I recently, against my better judgment, participated briefly in a Facebook conversation in which one person challenged anyone in general (and me in particular) to provide "one single, solid piece of evidence that he or she has ever had an encounter with God." It was very clear from the context of this challenge and the previous discussion that this person was defining "evidence" very narrowly—something tangible and objective that everyone could agree upon.

The evidence that grounds my faith is not of that sort. As it says in Hebrews, "Faith is the substance of things hoped for, the evidence of things

---

5. Hobbes, *Leviathan*, 76.

not seen."[6] What do I hope for? That there is a meaning to it all. That underneath the apparent chaos and meaninglessness of reality there is a vein of purpose that can be mined. Dorothy Allison puts it well:

> There is a place where we are always alone with our own mortality, where we must simply have something greater than ourselves to hold onto—God or history or politics or literature or a belief in the healing power of love, or even righteous anger. Sometimes I think they are all the same. A reason to believe, a way to take the world by the throat and insist that there is more to this life than we have ever imagined.[7]

My faith gives substance to this hope by encouraging me to accept all manner of things—experiences, intuitions, feelings—as "evidence" in support of the meaning and purpose I hope for that do not fit neatly within the very narrow definition of "evidence" that the Rust Cohles of the world insist upon. No better expression of an expanded openness to the abundant evidence related to hope has ever been written than in Shakespeare's *Hamlet*. When Horatio has difficulty believing that the ghost of Hamlet's father is real, Hamlet replies that "there are more things in heaven and earth, Horatio, than are dreamt of in your philosophy."[8] The best evidence that hopeful thinking is not magical thinking is a changed life. An encounter with the divine often can only be communicated on a "come and see" basis. In the Gospel of John, a formerly blind man whose sight has been restored by Jesus is grilled by the Pharisee authorities. Who did this? How did he do it? Don't you know that we have already concluded that this Jesus person is a sinner? The man simply responds "Whether He is a sinner or not I do not know. One thing I know: that though I was blind, now I see."[9] Experience trumps fact every time.

One Sunday during last year's Advent season the first reading was from the obscure prophet Zephaniah. The very name transports me back to my childhood where, as a dutiful five-year-old Baptist preacher's kid, I learned the names of the books of the Minor Prophets to an obnoxious singsongy tune. I could run through all of them in one breath—Hosea,

6. Heb 11:1.
7. Quoted in Rorty, *Philosophy*, 161.
8. Shakespeare, *Hamlet*, 1.5.167–68.
9. John 9:25.

Joel, Amos, Obadiah, Jonah, Micah, Nahum, Habakkuk, *Zephaniah*, Haggai, Zechariah, Malachi. These obscure texts were written in a distant time for a distant people in contexts and for reasons known only to the most narrowly focused academics. Yet there are memorable promises buried in these forgotten pages. Zephaniah's promise is: "I will bring you home."[10]

A friend who knows Jeanne and me well wrote in an email to me a few years ago that "you and Jeanne are home for each other." And it's a good thing. When her mother died in late 2002, the last of our four parents to pass away, Jeanne said to me "now we're orphans." Indeed, we were officially orphans, but we had felt as if we were orphans for most of the almost fifteen years at that time that we had been together. When Jeanne and I, along with my two sons (ages nine and six), set up housekeeping together for the first time in Milwaukee in August 1988, my parents were living over 1,000 miles to the west in Wyoming and Jeanne's parents were more than 1,000 miles to the east in Brooklyn. These distances deprived our new blended family of badly needed support and wisdom, a situation made even worse when my mother died of cancer within two months of our arrival in Wisconsin, followed unexpectedly by my father-in-law's passing just two weeks later. Jeanne read an article once listing a number of the top stress creators that a human being might go through in their lifetime, including changing jobs, moving, divorce, marriage, and the death of loved ones. We experienced all of them within the first tumultuous months of our relationship.

Although it would be another fourteen years before my father and mother-in-law died, Dad of heart failure and Rose after several years of descent into the hell of Alzheimer's, the distances between the two of us and our remaining parents never decreased. I learned immediately after my mother died the truth of what I had suspected all along—she was the one connecting thread that bound me tightly to my father, my brother, and other members of my extended family. Although Jeanne's mother and four siblings remained and would have helped if they could have, they were still over 1,000 miles away. For the day-to-day struggles of making our new family work, we were alone, often making it up as we went along. Which often seems to be the human condition—making it up as we go along.

Being an orphan is to be abandoned and alone. My father's favorite theologian, Jacques Ellul, once wrote a book entitled *Hope in Time of Abandonment*. The heart of this hope is expressed in a line from one of my favorite hymns: "Alleluia! Not as orphans are we left in sorrow now." The

---

10. Zeph 3:20.

promise and reality of redemption, that we are not alone, is throughout Scripture. But so often it sounds like a platitude—"I am with you always," "I will not leave you comfortless," "I will never leave you nor forsake you." Looks good on a plaque on the wall or on a bumper sticker, but when real life happens, the truth is in line with what a friend said to me once in the middle of a difficult time. "We come into the world alone and we leave the world alone." Hard words, but true.

But if we truly are not strangers in a strange land, if there truly is a home for each of us somewhere in this world of separation and alienation, that's great news. A manger in a barn is not much of a home, but it has served as the centering touchstone for countless persons because a home is far more than a location or a physical structure. At the heart of Advent is the outrageous promise that we humans and the divine belong together. The fourth-century church father Athanasius said "God became man so that man might become God." There's more in that claim than could be unpacked in a lifetime, but that's the mystery that Advent prepares us for—a cosmic homecoming.

At the other end of the liturgical year from Advent lies Easter. There is no shortage of material to consider on Easter—the empty tomb, Peter and John racing to take a look, the authorities scrambling to explain what happened, the poignant exchange between Mary Magdalene and Jesus. My favorite Easter-related story is Luke's account of the disciples on the road to Emmaus. It's such a human story—the bitter sadness and devastation of Cleopas and his unnamed companion (call him George) is palpable. The usual spin on the story is, of course, that Jesus is risen and walking with them, and Cleopas and George are either too dense or blinded by tears to know it's him. Jesus gives them a free theology lesson, and as soon as they recognize him after he breaks the bread at lunch, he vanishes. It says something (I'm not sure what) about me that I always thought the ending of the story was funny when I was young. Young Baptist boys have to get their laughs where they can find them. But three words are particularly resonant: "*We had hoped* that He was the one to redeem Israel."[11] This story is intimately personal, so representative of the crushed hopes and dreams, the inescapable pain and disappointment that are fundamentally part of the human experience. The events were devastating for those who were there,

---

11. Luke 24:21.

those who had tied their lives to this man. He had seemed to be something more, but turned out to be the same as everyone else—human, limited, subject to suffocating power and injustice, to the random events that ultimately shape each of our stories. We had hoped—and he died.

Every human life is marked by "we had hoped" moments that we never quite get over. I hoped that I would be a concert pianist. Jeanne hoped she would marry someone who knows how to dance. But the dashed hopes of Cleopas and George are far more crushing. It's easy to criticize Cleopas and George for failing to recognize that what they had hoped for was walking with them for seven miles, but that's not entirely fair. True, Jesus does turn out to "redeem Israel," and everybody else for that matter, but that's not the redemption Cleopas, George and others were hoping for, a political redemption and establishment of an earthly kingdom by the Messiah. And it's very telling that the Jesus-guided tour through the Jewish Scriptures touching on prophetic texts indicating that the Messiah would suffer and die doesn't do anything for Cleopas and George. It's not until the three of them have a meal, a human experience rather than a classroom experience, that they see it's been Jesus all the time.

In *Amazing Grace*, Kathleen Norris asks "Does it ever surprise you that God chooses to be revealed in so fallible a fashion?"[12] Yes, it does. All the time. Even when our greatest hopes are satisfied, it's always in some sideways, back door, behind the scenes, fuzzy and oblique sort of way. And that can be frustrating. Jesus' resurrection, for Christians the most spectacular and crucial event in human history, is surrounded by so many instances of mistaken identity, fumbling around, uncertainty, and missteps that it is truly comical.

But it makes perfect sense, and brings the central pillars of the Christian faith—the incarnation, the crucifixion, and the resurrection—together. The whole idea of incarnation, of God becoming human through and through, is outrageous and ludicrous at its core. What self-respecting creator of the universe would do it this way? Only one that loves what was created so much that becoming part of it, miraculously, is not only not a step down but is actually the only way to accomplish what has to be accomplished. We know that we are flawed, incomplete, jumbled and messed up creatures, so why should we be surprised that our hopes get addressed in that way? The divinely infused cycle of death and resurrection is everywhere in my daily life, in nature coming alive after a long winter, in church services populated

---

12. Norris, *Amazing Grace*, 135.

by octogenarians and toddlers, and in the annual arrival of new late teens ready to be taught on campus. It is not at all surprising that the resurrected Jesus, the hope of the world, was revealed in the midst of the daily and mundane rather than in power and glory. Kathleen Norris once again: "In a religion based on a human incarnation of the divine, when ideology battles experience, it is fallible, ordinary experience that must win."[13]

13. Ibid.

13

Incarnation—A Preposterous Love

I came to Minnesota to begin sabbatical in the middle of January. Throughout the winter, native Minnesotans kept promising that the ice would eventually leave Stumpf Lake and winter would give way to spring, although they didn't say that when May began most of the tree buds still would be buds. One native added that I would know when it would not snow again when the loons returned to the lake, because the loons never show up until the winter is over. Having no experience with loons, I had no idea whether this is a provable fact or yet another of the many tall tales I suspected the natives enjoy telling each new batch of outliers who live with them from semester to semester. And it isn't just Minnesotans who enjoy doing this. In the little Wyoming town in which I lived for a short while many years ago, there was a local watering hole called the Jackalope Café. The inside of the bar was a taxidermist's heaven, with mounted heads of buffalo, moose, bear, elk, deer, some sort of wild cat, and bighorn sheep crowding for space. Always seated at the bar was a collection of interesting human specimens, cowboys and ranchers who all were missing at least one body part—an eye, a finger, several teeth, something. Over the bar were other unusual specimens, the heads of what looked for all the world like large jackrabbits, but sporting horns. And not just any horns—they look just like the racks of pronghorn antelope.

These heads were from specimens of the West's most mysterious and elusive animal, the jackalope. A traveler can find evidence of the jackalope throughout the West, from the café in Afton, Wyoming to Jackalope Pottery in Santa Fe, New Mexico. In addition to the ubiquitous mounted jackalope heads, there are jackalope books, jackalope post cards, jackalope key rings, jackalope magnets, jackalope shot glasses, jackalope T-shirts—you get the idea. The regulars in the Jackalope Café had an endless supply of jackalope stories—how hard it is to find one, how elusive they are, their natural viciousness when cornered—stories that ratcheted up in complexity and detail when someone obviously from out of town walked through the door. There's nothing a rural Westerner enjoys more than astounding an Eastern city person with jackalope tales. Because as wonderful as the stories are, jackalopes don't exist. The heads on the wall really *are* jackrabbit heads with antelope horns stuck on top of them. They are the source of many laughs when yet another gullible rube from the East has been duped. But don't be too hard on the rubes—people in England thought that the preserved bodies of platypuses brought back from Australia were beavers or muskrats with duck bills sewn on them until they saw a live one. And anything that's as lucrative and entertaining as the jackalope must have some truth to it.

At least loons are real. I know they are, because they eventually returned to the lake (and it didn't snow after that, either). They showed up on a misty April morning, the morning *after* Jeanne's week-long Easter visit ended, a week during which she saw lots of little birds, a million squirrels, one eagle off in the distance, and no loons (or deer, fifteen of whom had an early morning breakfast picnic on the lawn in front of my apartment just *before* Jeanne came to visit). The morning the loon pair arrived, I heard their famous call. Later that day, upon hearing that I had seen and heard loons, one of my friends from Washington, DC, said, "I've never heard or seen a loon. What do they sound like?" To which I replied, "There's a reason for the saying 'crazy as a loon.' They sound like an insane woman's laugh."

Loons and jackalopes. Although there's a significant ontological difference between them, it's probably just a quirk of natural selection that there are no horned bunnies. Maybe there were giant prehistoric carnivorous jackalopes who were the bane of the earth, who became extinct along with the dinosaurs for still unknown reasons. Why not? Horned rabbits don't strike me as any less possible than water birds with long necks who sound like the Wicked Witch of the West. Annie Dillard puts it this way: "Look, in short, at practically anything—the coot's feet, the mantis's face, a banana, the human ear—and see that not only did the creator create everything, but

Incarnation—A Preposterous Love

he is apt to create *anything*. He'll stop at nothing."[1] The natural world looks less like intelligent design and more like an explosion of exuberance.

"He'll stop at nothing"—that's a pretty good summary of God's dealings with us. The poet Kilian MacDonnell writes of "Our preposterous God with a preposterous love,"[2] and that's just the right word for it. In stories from the Jewish Scriptures, time after time I can hear God sighing, "Okay, people, let's try this *again*. Just do this handful of things, and everything will be fine." Then, of course, it gets messed up, God tries again, gets pissed off but doesn't give up, and so on. Then God has an idea so out of the box, so off the radar, that it's ludicrous in its originality. "I'll become human." In a novel I finished recently, a character was explaining her decision not to convert from Christianity to Judaism when she married.

> The great appeal of Jesus is the willingness of God to walk among the benighted creatures He just can't seem to give up on. There is a glorious looniness to it—the magnificent eternal gesture of salvation, in the face of perennial, thickheaded human inanity! I like that in a deity.

So do I.[3]

As a young boy, I was thoroughly confused by the idea that Jesus was simultaneously divine and human. It didn't help that while the authorities in church said this, Jesus' divine nature was emphasized so strongly at the expense of his humanity that for me Jesus became God wearing a human Halloween costume—looked and acted human, but really wasn't. When I got to college and started studying philosophy, I learned that philosophers have historically also had a difficult time figuring out how the various parts of a human being fit together; one of the most popular "go-to" models is that a human being is a physical thing (body) plus something else (soul/mind) that is not physical. Furthermore, according to some of the greats such as Plato, Augustine, and Descartes, the "something else" is where the most important part of the human resides—the body is essentially a temporary vehicle in which the immortal soul gets carried around for a time. This model is called "dualism" and is scandalously problematic in philosophy. Early Christian doctrine adopted a dualistic model of the human person,

---

1. Dillard, *Pilgrim*, 136.
2. MacDonnell, *God Drops*, 60.
3. Russell, *Children*, 264.

introducing equally scandalous problems into its framework, such as the idea that the body is a bad thing, that we are strangers in the physical world, and that the goal of the Christian life is to survive sufficiently intact to make it to heaven after physical death.

Dualism not only offers a skewed and problematic map of reality, but also fundamentally contorts and deforms the very heart and soul of Christian belief—the incarnation. If believing that God became human means anything, it is that the greatest and most cosmic dualistic split of all—the one between human and divine—has been healed. The divine response to human failings is not to cover them up but rather to transform the human by infusing it with the divine. The promise of incarnation is all about immanence—God with (and in) us. It sometimes surprises my students to learn that "incarnation" literally means "to become meat." Carnivore, carnivorous, chili con carne, carnal. Or to put it differently, "incarnation" means "to put skin on." God's response to human need, sorrow, pain, and suffering is to wrap the divine up in flesh. On a given day, in a given situation, that incarnated God might be me. It might be you. This is how the divine chooses to be in the world. God is a person with skin on.

As I suspect is the case with many Protestants, I never knew exactly what to do with Mary; a good friend and longtime Presbyterian minister told me not long ago that he could never convert to Catholicism because "I just don't get that Mary thing." But there's no denying that the story of the annunciation is a game changer. In Scripture, angels are always the heralds of new beginnings, inviting us to adventure. They introduce mystery—they do not clarify. Angels announce new departures and the origins of something whose end is not in view. The angel Gabriel's announcement to Mary is an explosion of beauty from the first sentence: "Greetings, favored one! The Lord is with you."[4] We are all very aware of our humanity, of our shortcomings and failings. But the promise of incarnation is that God chooses, inexplicably, miraculously, to inhabit flawed and imperfect matter, to become human. The promise to Mary is the promise to us—the Lord is with us. We, as Mary, are the wombs from which the divine enters the world each day. We are the incubators of God. Mary's response to Gabriel is the only one possible—"How can this be?"[5] It is a mystery. It is also a great story.

When Mary gathers herself sufficiently to comment on the angel's announcement after he leaves, she begins in the right place. "For he has looked

---

4. Luke 1:28.
5. Luke 1:34.

Incarnation—A Preposterous Love

with favor on the lowliness of his servant. Surely, from now on all generations will call me blessed."[6] Mary is saying that "I'm nothing special. I'm just a garden-variety human being. But the divine has showed favor toward me and has bestowed abundant blessing on me by choosing to inhabit me." There is only one possible reason for this favor, because Mary knows that she has done nothing to earn it. This reason is love. Love is holy because it is a lot like grace—the worthiness of its object is never really what matters. The astounding mystery and wonder of God's love for us permeates throughout the beautiful story of the annunciation. This favor and blessing continues. The incarnation narrative—the story of God becoming flesh—is a direct response to our inherent flaws, imperfections, limitations, and evil. Divine favor and blessing is offered to all of us. And the status of humanity is raised when God inhabits it. I remember singing a Sunday school song as a child that included the lines "we are his hands, we are his feet." That is the mystery, the scandal, and the beauty of the incarnation story: God entrusts flawed human beings to be the divine in the world.

At St. John's University and Abbey in Collegeville, Minnesota, Benedictine priest Godfrey Diekmann was a rock star. He and his mentor, Fr. Virgil Michael, were perhaps more responsible for the liturgical reform and renewal in the Catholic Church that emerged from Vatican II than any others. Godfrey Diekmann stories abound—his wit and temper were legendary. One evening while eating with colleagues and students in the student cafeteria, Diekmann got involved in a spirited conversation about the heart of Christian theology and life. He startled those at his table as well as those within earshot by slamming his hand on the table and shouting "It's not the resurrection, god-dammit! It's the incarnation!" As students, stunned into silence, slipped away, he added, "But we don't believe it. We don't believe that we are invited to become the very life of God." The incarnation is the moment of salvation as God enters time, history, and each of us.

Advent's strongest image is pregnancy. Elizabeth's . . . Mary's . . . so unexpected, so miraculous. Advent reminds us that in our lives there is always a child ready to enter the world—the divine child that is in each of us and the child of God that each of us is. We are favored of God, loved by God, regardless of whether we feel it or deserve it. A great gift has been placed in us, a gift that carries with it unlimited responsibility. How will we nurture this child? How will we bring it to birth? What is incubating in each of us is as individual and unique as each of us is—and it is divine. How will

---

6. Luke 1:48.

we welcome this child? Mary's response must be ours: "Here we are, the servants of the Lord. Let it be with us according to your Word."

God begets his Son in you whether you like it or not, whether you sleep or wake—still God is at work.[7] —Meister Eckhart

A baptism is occasionally part of the morning service in the Episcopal Church. One recent Sunday there were two baptisms—ten-year-old Brooke and her two-year-old brother Jacob. Many moons ago, when I was in my twenties and considering joining the Episcopal Church, their practice of baptizing young children, even infants, gave me pause. So much about the Episcopal way of doing things was attractive and an obvious spiritual balm to the scars I carried in my twenties from my conservative, fundamentalist upbringing. Liturgy, a pipe organ, excellent music, clerical robes, a prayer book, weekly Eucharist—if I had been aware enough to design worship that spoke to my deepest aesthetic and spiritual needs, it would have been exactly like Sunday morning at St. Matthew's Cathedral.

But they baptized infants. After finishing the baptismal liturgy, the Dean would carry the baby up and down the center aisle of the cathedral, saying "This is the brand-newest Christian in the world!" as the congregation applauded. For someone taught from his earliest memory that becoming a Christian involved a "born-again experience," a once-for-all conversion event that required a certain level of rational maturity and spiritual awareness, this business of becoming a Christian simply by some water being poured on one's head in the manner specified by the prayer book was jarring. My own full-immersion baptism, performed by my father in a swimming pool-sized baptismal font when I was twelve, was what a baptism is supposed to be like. I've always thought, despite sacred art and Hollywood depictions, that John the Baptist did not just pour a bit of water on Jesus' head that day in the Jordan River—he dunked him.

None of this stopped me from being confirmed as an Episcopalian more than twenty-five years ago, as I chose to embrace a bit of spiritual life and comfort where I found it. And I'm still not sure about what's going on at a baptism. But as I watched and participated as a member of the congregation in these two baptisms, I was struck by the obvious pleasure that the young girl, dressed entirely in white, was taking in the proceedings.

---

7. Eckhart, *Meister Eckhart*, 5.

I heard the beautiful words toward the end of the baptismal liturgy—"You are marked as Christ's own forever." My doctrinal issues with baptizing children dissolved into a puddle of irrelevance.

Shortly after, as Jeanne and I were headed toward the altar for communion, the brand-newest Christian in the world was making her way down the steps after having received the body and blood of Christ for the first time in her life. As she walked by us, she looked in our direction, screwed up her face, and said in a loud stage whisper, "I don't like it!" Out of the mouths of babes. "Kid, you don't know the half of it," I thought. There are going to be many things upcoming that you'll dislike a lot more than a communion wafer epoxied to the roof of your mouth and the aftertaste of cheap wine. This "marked as Christ's own forever" stuff is no picnic.

In the past, I've heard police and firefighter work described as 95 percent boredom and 5 percent sheer terror. That's something like my experience over several decades of being one of "Christ's own forever." There have been long stretches of my life when there were no identifiable signs of such a privilege. The problem with ordinary spiritual commitment, as I've experienced it and heard it described by others, is that it is so ordinary as to be unnoticeable. Sure, there have been some "Big Bird moments" where the divine broke through so obviously that even I could not mistake it. But what about the weeks, months, and years during which those who are marked as Christ's own forever slog through the barren desert of the everyday and mundane? Sometimes the silence is so deafening and the absence so palpable that the value of belonging to Christ escapes me. Teresa of Avila once complained to God that "If this is the way you treat your friends, it's no wonder you have so few." No kidding—I don't like it.

In one of Iris Murdoch's novels, a central character has a vision in which she is visited in her kitchen by Jesus. As he leaves the room after a brief conversation, Jesus touches the woman on the hand. When the vision ends, she knows that her experience was not simply imaginary because her hand is painfully burned where Jesus touched her. Although the burn heals, and the pain eventually fades over the following days, a small but permanent scar remains. For the rest of her life her scar is an indelible reminder that she is forever changed because one day she encountered Jesus.[8]

Perhaps baptism is something like that. Somewhere in the past and continuing history of those who are scarred by the mark of Christ are events, people, decisions, and experiences that form the skeleton, the

---

8. Murdoch, *Nuns and Soldiers*, 280–86.

internal structure of faith. A person's spiritual identity is shaped by this structure, fleshed out in ways unique to each individual. Some pieces of this identity come out of the blue, divinely tinged experiences that cannot be easily accommodated or dismissed. Others are deliberately chosen, such as a baptism, responding to an altar call, a choice of worship community, or turning away from what no longer gives life. As Brooke's and Jacob's lives as one of Christ's own unfold, each will be able to identify their baptismal Sunday as a signpost of difference. The fact that Brooke was part of the decision-making process while Jacob's loving family chose the time and place of his baptism for him is not crucially important. The imprint of the divine on a human life often has nothing to do with individual choice.

The beauty of the incarnation is that each of the moments of all of our days are full of divine beauty and grace. The beauty is not in the product, the greatness of what I or anyone, marked as Christ's own, might become or achieve. The beauty is not even in the gloriously random Big Bird experiences that leaven our lives. The beauty is in the very idea of God in the flesh, an indwelling reality that sanctifies even our most mundane days and disturbing experiences. "Marked as Christ's own forever"—that's something to embrace, even when I don't like it.

A disturbingly common mishap in recent Summer Olympic Games has been the failure of US track and field relay teams. Individually, these teams almost always include the best runners, top to bottom, that our country has to offer. Best times, best individual win-loss records. But great individuals do not a successful relay team make. In a relay race, each runner is required not only to run her or his lap as swiftly as possible, but also to hand the baton to the next runner smoothly and securely within a specified number of meters. As the baton falls to the track during these attempted transfers, time after time, the truth becomes crystal clear. In the quintessential American spirit, the members of the US relay teams have spent far too much time honing their individual running skills, and far too little time practicing how to be a team (if they've practiced at all). Passing a baton while both the baton passer and receiver are running, one decelerating and one accelerating, within a limited amount of space, takes practice, practice that is not nearly as sexy or stimulating as running as fast as one can by oneself.

Baton passing serves as an interesting analogy for many human situations, particularly generational ones that involve passing a virtual baton from the geezers to the young punks. A successful transfer requires the ability and desire to receive and run on the younger generation's part and a willingness to let go and to slow down from the older veterans. Debate about curriculum reform swirled around my campus for many years, centering on a large, twenty-credit-hour course, described as the "core of the core" at my college, a course that is required of all freshmen and sophomores. This course was created in the early 1970s; it was groundbreaking and audacious in its day. Many of the faculty who were the "young Turks" of that day, the movers and shakers who invented this course and shepherded it through the faculty senate and administration against all odds, are now senior faculty on the verge of retirement. Others have already retired, some have passed away. And the course they created, which defined many of their academic careers both in the classroom and out, became stale and badly in need of fresh vision and creative reconstruction.

Despite the good will of many of the next generation of younger faculty, highly qualified and motivated women and men who willingly seek to carry a revitalized course forward for the next few decades, the reform debate was frequently poisoned by resistance to any meaningful change by the older generation. It was sad to observe. By accident of age and time served at the college I was positioned, as both one of the youngest of the older generation and one of the most experienced of the new generation, at the very point where the baton transfer should have occurred. As a veteran of teaching in this program and a long-standing advocate for needed change, I was asked to direct the new version of the program that emerged from curriculum reform through its transition from the past into the future. I told several of my senior colleagues over the subsequent months, "it's impossible to run a relay race if you won't let go of the baton."

A number of years ago Ascension Sunday happened to be the seventeenth and last Sunday that I would be worshipping at St. John's Abbey in Collegeville, Minnesota on sabbatical. As I sat in my choir stall seat during seven o'clock morning prayer, then in the sanctuary later in the morning during mass, there was a certain wistfulness and a bit of emotion, but not as much as I expected. For this Ascension Sunday was an appropriate milestone in my spiritual growth, a marker of the point at which I would tentatively and with fear and trembling take what I had learned and experienced over the previous four months "into all the world." I was never taught to pay attention to Ascension Sunday in my religious tradition. Even after I was introduced to the liturgical calendar for the first time in my middle twenties,

Ascension Sunday was simply the Sunday before Pentecost, after which we would slog through week after week of Ordinary Time boredom in green through the summer and fall until we were rescued by Advent purple right after Thanksgiving. But as I inhabited for the first time the Psalms and New Testament texts on that Ascension Sunday, I thought, "Wow. Jesus was the ultimately prepared and successful baton passer."

Ascension Sunday completes the story of the incarnation that began with Jesus' birth. Jesus doesn't ascend out of his human body to heaven—he takes it with him, because the next lap of this story, the "Christ in us" lap, is just about ready to explode. Jesus showed extraordinary patience with his all-too-human followers during his short stay on earth, teaching them basic truths through stories and actions, all preparation for when it would be up to them to receive the baton and run their own incarnational race. The forty days after the resurrection were all practice for a smooth passing of the baton. Jesus kept telling them, "It's alright. I'm not leaving you alone. It's better for you that I go, because I'll be sending you the greatest teammate ever. You can do this, because I'll still be with you. When I leave, don't go crazy and start running in every direction out of fear or impatience. Wait. Pray. You'll know when it's time to run. And when you do, you'll turn the world upside down." And when the clouds closed on Jesus' heels as he ascended into heaven, for once the men and women who had loved and followed him did what they were told. They went into an upper room in Jerusalem and waited.

I'm told that the receiver of the baton in a relay race should not seek to accelerate until she or he feels the slap of the baton in the palm of the receiving hand they have extended backwards as they begin to run. The receiver never sees the runner coming up behind, but there's no mistaking the transfer from the unseen runner when it happens. And in the upper room ten days after Jesus left, there was no mistaking that the baton had been successfully transferred. The incarnation goes on, and we recipients of the Holy Spirit carry it "to the ends of the earth." In his Ascension Sunday homily, the abbott observed that with Ascension Day, the Easter message of "Glory, Glory, Glory" that has been front and center for forty days changes to "Go!" The word to me that day and ever since was "Take what you've been given, what you've found, and go." We are carrying the baton, and are to run as if our lives depended on it. Because they do.

Conclusion

Learning How to Read

On one of my family's summer western treks, we pulled into a Phillips 66 station to fill up. "What does the 66 stand for?" my dad asked, to which I immediately replied "the sixty-six books of the Bible?" "Right," he said. Although I found out many years later that this is not true, don't blame my dad for feeding me false information. Many people thought that the number in Phillips 66 came from the books of the Bible, and the founder of Phillips Petroleum Company didn't straighten people out about the name's origin for years. Good publicity to keep people guessing; as it turns out, the number was chosen to reflect the excitement of Route 66 being constructed across the heartland into the West. One of the first facts I learned about the Bible is how many books it contained. And I knew them cold. In Sunday school, we little Baptists learned songs whose lyrics were the books of the Bible in order as soon as we learned to talk (usually before we learned to read). At Bible camp one year there was a girl who could say the books of the Bible backwards (all of us could say them in correct order). I didn't exactly see what the practical applications of that skill might be, but it was impressive.

Once we got a bit older, around ten or so, we learned another skill in Sunday school: how to find any verse in the Bible as quickly as possible. To hone this skill, we had competitions called "sword drills," since Paul calls the word of God the "sword of the spirit" in Ephesians.[1] Our teacher would say "draw your swords," and we would raise our Bibles with one hand above our heads. Each of us had brought ours from home, of course—I

---

1. Eph 6:17.

don't know what would have happened to someone who forgot their Bible, since I don't recall it ever happening. The teacher would call out a Bible reference—book, chapter, and verse—and then, after a tantalizing pause, would shout "*Go!*" Whoever found the Scripture and started reading it first won. And I was good. I mean *really* good. I had a cousin who used to win infrequently (maybe once every ten times), but other than that it was all me all the time. If the teacher said "John 3:16!" I would roll my eyes and think "Please. That's in the Gospels. I know that one by heart—give us something challenging." "Psalms 101:11!" "Come on, I can win that with one hand tied behind my back." "Micah 6:8!" "Lamentations 4:2!" "Habakkuk 3:17!" "Now you're talking," I thought, as I got the verse then waited a moment, just to make things interesting, while my fellow sword wielders fumbled around, reading the verse just as the kid next to me was getting ready to read it. "Now we're separating the real sword masters from the wannabes." "Hezekiah 17:32!" I watched my comrades with disdain as they plowed into their swords, pitying them and how foolish they would feel when they found out it was a trick command—there is no book of Hezekiah in the Bible. I wasn't very good at traditional sports like football and basketball, but man I could wield a sword.

So imagine my reaction—dismay, shock, outrage—when I found out that some people (who shall remain nameless) added some extra books to the Bible, jammed in between the Old and New Testaments. I can remember exactly when it happened. In the late sixties and early seventies (my junior high and high school years), several new translations of the Bible came out. This was disturbing enough, since in my crowd "King James" was not the star of the Cleveland Cavaliers—"King James" was the name of the only authoritative translation of the Bible. We were taught to believe that the Bible is the inerrant word of God; no one corrected us when we additionally assumed that God had dictated the book in King James English. But when I looked in one of these new translations and saw a bunch of unfamiliar books under the collective title "The Apocrypha," I thought "What the hell is this?" "First and Second Maccabees"? "Baruch"? "The Song of the Three Men"? "Tobit"? That sounds like something from Tolkien: "In a hole in the ground lived a tobit." "Bel and the Dragon"? What's that, a comic book? I didn't know what to think, except that someone had been messing around with my Bible, and I was pissed.

I have to admit that, although it's now more than forty years later, I've never read any of these apocryphal books in their entirety. There are some

Conclusion

bits and pieces of these books in the Episcopal prayer book as canticles for morning and evening prayer, which isn't surprising since we Episcopalians are willing to appropriate anything from any tradition so long as it is good liturgy, fine music, or profound literature, always assuming that it will also support a liberal, left-leaning mind-set. But I feel a bit odd reading parts of "The Song of the Three" or "The Prayer of Manasseh," as if I'm doing something wrong. Old habits and beliefs die hard, especially when they were established in the cradle.

I stopped believing that the Bible is the inerrant, literal word of God while still in my teens, and have occasionally wondered since then exactly what the Bible is for me now. It is part of my tradition, my heritage, and my history. I am forever grateful that I had the opportunity, although often a forced one, to make its stories, its poetry, its history, part of my intellectual foundation at a very early age—foundations laid at such an age remain largely intact. I rely on that foundation every day in the classroom and during outside-of-class conversations with students and colleagues. It is a shared touchstone in Jeanne's and my life. And I still am thoroughly comfortable with calling it the word of God—but what exactly does that mean?

I recall a memorable Sunday evening in my early twenties when a venerable Bible scholar, an elder at the large church my family was attending and the godfather of my then six-month-old firstborn son, stood behind the pulpit, raised his Bible above eye level for all to see (almost like a sword drill) and said with great courage to a largely evangelical congregation: "This is not the word of God! This is a bunch of pages between leather covers written by human beings. It becomes the word of God when the Holy Spirit writes its message in your heart. Remember, the letter kills, but the Spirit gives life." Other than a gasp or two, you could have heard a pin drop.

But he was right. As I've returned to the texts of my youth over the past several years in both communal and private reading, new life has risen in me. In the Benedictine daily cycle of prayers, noon prayer always begins with several verses from Psalm 119, which is the longest chapter in the Bible and is all about the glories of God's word. The psalmist never says a thing about the written word—God's word always is hidden in our hearts, written in our minds, lived out in our actions. And as my son's godfather implied, the Spirit can transform anything, any text, written or otherwise, into the word of God. The Bible in my experience is special because it is at the heart of what I believe and its words have become God's word for me more often than any other source. But it could be Shakespeare. Or Nietzsche. Or

Jeanne. Or my dachshund. Or the sun rising this morning—in a sacramental world, anything can be the word of God. Even Tobit, I suppose.

My early years were full of stories of how I learned to read. According to my mother, I was reading by age three without anyone teaching me how to do it. I was never without a book. I lined my menagerie of stuffed animals up on the couch and read to them. Knowing how stories tend to take on a life of their own, I cannot attest to the accuracy of these reports (although it was my father rather than my mother who was prone to telling tall tales). I do know that my love of books extends as far back as I can remember, and that I knew how to read before I could tell time or tie my shoes—perhaps my parents should have provided me with instruction manuals to read. Because I could read on a fifth-grade level before starting first grade, according to the local school board member who tested me at home, I went through first and second grade in one year, moving from first to second grade (in the same room in our tiny school) after Christmas break. I've paid a lifelong price for that honor—I joined second grade when they were all the way to the letter "W" in their cursive writing studies. My "w's" "x's," "y's" and "z's" are fabulous, but other than that my cursive has been illegible, even to me, ever since.

Several years ago during an eye exam, my new ophthalmologist asked "do you read very much?" I laughed as I said "I read for a living!" The written word is not only the foundation of my professional life, but has also been my spiritual lifeline since childhood. For many years all that remained of my religious upbringing was the Bible. Even though I no longer believed it to be the literally inerrant word of God, as I was taught, large portions of it resided in my memory, ready to be accessed in class and conversation as well as popping up even when uninvited. I memorized large portions of the Bible growing up, as all good Baptist kids should, always reminded that "Thy Word have I hid in my heart, that I might not sin against Thee."[2] We were taught that since the canon of Scripture was completed, we should not expect further communication from the divine in the form of miracles, signs and wonders, or direct communication. We already had God's final word to us in completed form; now we just needed to obey it and hang on until the second coming.

---

2. Psa 119:11 KJV.

Conclusion

Theologian Patrick Henry writes that "God died because people forgot how to read."[3] I was reminded of his claim a while ago as I read a manuscript on Simone Weil's philosophy as an outside reader for an academic press. She argues that we "read" everything in our environment—that reading is always and immediately a matter of interpretation. "The sky, the sea, the sun, the stars, human beings, everything that surrounds us is . . . something that we read."[4] This is a much broader understanding of "reading" than our traditional Western conception, which describes reading as an exclusively cognitive, intellectual, and mental activity—precisely the sort of activity I've spent the majority of my waking hours on this planet doing. So how is it that such a crucial, human-defining activity as reading could be forgotten, even to the point of emptying the divine of content? The problem is not with reading per se—it's that we've forgotten that reading is not just an intellectual activity. God's death is not due to a misuse of or over-reliance on the activity of reading. It's due to forgetting what true reading even is.

I had heard and read about "lectio divina"—sacred reading—for years, but it had not struck me as a particularly interesting concept. Just another skill to learn, technique to master, perhaps—but really, reading is one thing I know how to do pretty well. But after several weeks of daily prayer with the abbey monks, it dawned on me that lectio divina isn't about words, meaning, or retention at all. I often found that I did not remember, even for the amount of time it took to walk from the choir stalls to the front of the abbey and exit, which Psalms we had read nor any of the content. Yet I had a sense that what we were doing was far more important than reading a book, marking it with highlighter and pen in my usual method, and perhaps memorizing a phrase or two for future reference in class or conversation.

What was happening in the choir stalls was not exclusively a mind event, but a full body experience bypassing my overdeveloped mind and seeping into all the other parts of me that had been starved for years. My bodily rhythms, my intuitions, my emotions, my spirit. The Psalms speak of God's word all the time, but almost never of *thinking about* God's word. It's more like what Jeremiah reports: "Your words were found, and I ate them, and your words became to me a joy and the delight of my heart."[5] Simone Weil was channeling her internal Jeremiah when she wrote that "I only read

---

3. Henry, *Ironic*, 70.
4. Weil, *Simone Weil*, 23.
5. Jer 15:16.

what I am hungry for at the moment when I have an appetite for it, and then I do not read, I *eat*."[6] And like a mother bird regurgitating food for the babies, an important word or phrase would come into my consciousness later in the day, one that I didn't remember reading but which had dripped into my soul.

In our "real world" of immediacy, getting it done, making money and a living, is there a place for what I began to absorb in a Benedictine abbey in middle-of-nowhere Minnesota? Over the subsequent years I've seen small but important evidence of change in how I converse with people, how I approach the day, and a heightened and more immediate sense of when a layer is threatening to grow back over my divine reading space. Learning how to read differently is not just another technique; rather, it is a new way of being and is transferable to everything. I went on sabbatical expecting to write about trying to sustain a life of faith when God at best is a silent partner who never writes, calls, emails, texts, or tweets. Now the divine is everywhere and seems to have a lot to say. Reading the divine begins with believing that everything is sacramental, infused with the breath of God, with taking "the Word became flesh" very seriously. All of creation is a sacred text. I didn't know it, because I didn't know how to read.

Outside the windows of my sabbatical apartment, windows which stretched from floor to ceiling along the entire width of the south side of the apartment, was a beautiful lake. Over the months I lived there, I watched hundreds of birds of dozens of sorts alight on this lake, stay for a while, and then move on. Sometimes they just floated for a while before flying away. Sometimes they plunged beneath the surface for an uncomfortably long time, then popped up far on the other side of the lake. A few I saw only once; maybe they found a better, more private lake where people aren't staring at them all the time. But the people who are permanent Minnesota residents rather than a visitor as I was say that there are some pairs of birds—all sorts of ducks, loons, grebes, Canadian geese, eagles—who come back every year. For at least a part of every year, Stumpf Lake in Collegeville, Minnesota is their home.

These days I think of the life of faith as being like this lake. I spent time on this lake as a young child, and had no idea it was this big. The portion I thought was the whole world turns out to be the shallow part of one corner

---

6. Weil, *Waiting*, 27.

Conclusion

of the lake. Upon return, I'm discovering depths that no one's ever found the bottom of. I've never been a big fan of the water, and I'm not a very good swimmer. But I'm getting better at it, and I don't need blow-up water wings to stay afloat any more. Annie Dillard describes this place well.

> I know only enough of God to want to worship him, by any means ready to hand. There is an anomalous specificity to all our experience in space, a scandal of particularity, by which God burgeons up or showers down into the shabbiest of occasions, and leaves his creation's dealings with him in the hands of purblind and clumsy amateurs.[7]

If the stories in the Bible have any truth to them, apparently God has an inexplicable love for "purblind and clumsy amateurs"—just look at the disciples and others who followed Jesus. Just look at me and everyone else I know who is trying the Christian incarnational narrative on for size. The only people who regularly annoyed Jesus were the people who professed to be something *other* than clumsy amateurs in matters of faith. But the root of "amateur" is "*amator*," the Latin word for "lover." And that's what I find here—a love that will not let me go. I find that to be amazing.

---

7. Dillard, *Pilgrim*, 55.

Bibliography

Bolz-Weber, Nadia. *Accidental Saints*. New York: Convergent, 2015.
———. *Pastrix*. New York: Jericho, 2013.
The Book of Common Prayer. New York: Seabury, 1979.
Borg, Marcus. *Convictions*. New York: HarperOne, 2014.
———. *Putting Away Childish Things*. New York: HarperCollins, 2010.
Cahill, Thomas. *The Gifts of the Jews*. New York: Anchor, 1998.
Camus, Albert. *The Myth of Sisyphus and Other Essays*. Translated by Justin O'Brien. New York: Vintage International, 1991.
———. *The Plague*. Translated by Stuart Gilbert. New York: Vintage International, 1991.
Chittister, Joan. *Essential Writings*. Edited by Mary Lou Kownacki and Mary Hembrow Snyder. Maryknoll, NY: Orbis, 2014.
———. *Wisdom Distilled from the Daily*. New York: HarperCollins, 1991.
Chittister, Joan, and Rowan Williams. *Uncommon Gratitude*. Collegeville, MN: Liturgical, 2010.
Dickinson, Emily. *The Complete Poems of Emily Dickinson*. Edited by Thomas H. Johnson. Boston: Back Bay, 1976.
Dillard, Annie. *For the Time Being*. New York: Vintage, 2000.
———. *Holy the Firm*. New York: Harper Perennial, 1998.
———. *Pilgrim at Tinker Creek*. New York: Harper Perennial, 2007.
———. *Teaching a Stone to Talk*. New York: Harper Perennial, 1988.
Drndić, Daša. *Trieste*. New York: Houghton Mifflin Harcourt, 2014.
Eckhart, Meister. *Meister Eckhart, from Whom God Hid Nothing*. Boston: New Seeks, 1996.
Eisenstein, Sergei. *Film Form: Essays in Film Theory*. New York: Harvest, 1969.
Eliot, George. *Middlemarch*. New York: Barnes and Noble Classics, 2003.
Francis (Pope). *Laudato Si': On Care for Our Common Home*. Mahwah, NJ: Paulist, 2015.
Gutting, Gary, and Louise Antony. "Arguments Against God." http://opinionator.blogs.nytimes.com/2014/02/25/arguments-against-god/.
Hampl, Patricia. *I Could Tell You Stories*. New York: W. W. Norton and Co., 1999.
Haught, John. *God After Darwin*. Boulder, CO: Westview, 2008.
Hawthorne, Nathaniel. *The Great Stone Face: And Other Tales of the White Mountains*. New York: Boomer, 2008.
Henry, Patrick G. *The Ironic Christian's Companion*. New York: Riverhead, 1999.

Bibliography

Henry, Patrick. *We Only Know Men*. Washington, DC: The Catholic University of America Press, 2013.
Hobbes, Thomas. *Leviathan*. Indianapolis: Hackett, 1994.
Hopkins, Gerard Manley. *Gerard Manley Hopkins: The Major Works*. Oxford: Oxford University Press, 2009.
Kahneman, Daniel. *Thinking, Fast and Slow*. New York: Farrar, Straus and Giroux, 2011.
Kidd, Susan Monk. *When the Heart Waits*. New York: HarperOne, 2006.
Kierkegaard, Søren. *Philosophical Fragments*. Princeton, NJ: Princeton University Press, 1974.
Kurtz, Ernest, and Katherine Ketcham. *The Spirituality of Imperfection*. New York: Bantam, 1992.
Kushner, Lawrence. *Kabbalah: A Love Story*. New York: Broadway, 2006.
Lamott, Anne. *Bird By Bird*. New York: Anchor, 1995.
———. *Plan B: Further Thoughts On Faith*. New York: Riverhead, 2005.
———. *Small Victories: Spotting Improbable Moments of Grace*. New York: Riverhead, 2014.
Lewis, C. S. *Letters to Malcolm: Chiefly on Prayer*. New York: Mariner, 2001.
———. *Yours, Jack*. Edited by Paul F. Ford. New York: HarperCollins, 2008.
Lightman, Alan. "Our Place in the Universe." http://harpers.org/archive/2012/12/our-place-in-the-universe/.
MacDonnell, Kilian. *God Drops and Loses Things*. Collegeville, MN: St. John's University Press, 2009.
Mantel, Hilary. *Wolf Hall*. London: Picador, 2010.
Martel, Yann. *Life of Pi*. Orlando: Harcourt, 2008.
Montaigne, Michel de. *Apology for Raymond Sebond*. Translated by Roger Ariew and Marjorie Grene. Indianapolis: Hackett, 2003.
———. *The Essays: A Selection*. Translated by M. A. Screech. London: Penguin, 1993.
Murdoch, Iris. *Existentialists and Mystics*. Edited by Peter Conradi. New York: Penguin, 1999.
———. *Metaphysics as a Guide to Morals*. New York: Penguin, 1992.
———. *Nuns and Soldiers*. New York: Penguin, 1980.
Newman, John Cardinal Henry. *Apologia Pro Vita Sua*. London: Sheed & Ward, 1948.
Norris, Kathleen, *Amazing Grace*. New York: Riverhead, 1999.
———. *The Cloister Walk*. New York: Riverhead, 1996.
O'Connor, Flannery. *The Complete Stories*. New York: Farrar, Strauss, and Giroux, 1971.
Pascal, Blaise. *Pensées*. Edited and translated by Roger Ariew. Indianapolis: Hackett, 2005.
Robinson, Marilynne. *Gilead*. New York: Picador, 2004.
———. *When I Was a Child I Read Books*. New York: Farrar, Strauss and Giroux, 2012.
Rorty, Richard. *Philosophy and Social Hope*. New York: Penguin, 1999.
Russell, Mary Doria. *Children of God*. New York: Ballantine, 1999.
Shakespeare, William. *Hamlet*. New York: Bantam Classic, 1988.
———. *King Lear*. New York: Bantam Classic, 2005.
Taylor, Barbara Brown. *An Altar in the World*. New York: HarperCollins, 2009.
———. *Leaving Church*. New York: HarperCollins, 2006.
———. *When God Is Silent*. Lanham, MD: Rowman & Littlefield, 1998.
Teilhard de Chardin, Pierre. *Christianity and Evolution*. New York: Harcourt, 1974.
Tippett, Krista. *Einstein's God*. New York: Penguin, 2010.

Bibliography

Tippett, Krista, and Arnold Eisen. "The Spiritual Audacity of Abraham Joshua Heschel." http://www.onbeing.org/program/spiritual-audacity-abraham-joshua-heschel/particulars/2267.

Tippett, Krista, and Anne Lamott. "The Meaning of Faith." http://www.onbeing.org/program/the-meaning-of-faith/transcript/6969.

Tippett, Krista, and Fatemeh Keshavarz. "The Ecstatic Faith of Rumi." http://www.onbeing.org/program/ecstatic-faith-rumi/transcript/2324.

Tippett, Krista, and Rami Nashashibi. "A New Coming Together." http://onbeing.org/program/rami-nashashibi-a-new-coming-together/transcript/7738#main_content.

Tolstoy, Leo. *War and Peace*. Translated by Louise and Aylmer Maude. Oxford: Oxford University Press, 2010.

Udin, Sala. "I Want to be a Freedom Rider." http://themoth.org/posts/stories/i-want-to-be-a-freedom-rider.

Weil, Simone. *Gravity and Grace*. Translated by Emma Craufurd. London: Routledge & Kegan Paul, 1972.

———. *The Need for Roots*. Translated by Arthur Wills. London: Routledge & Kegan Paul, 2002.

———. *The Notebooks of Simone Weil*. 2 vols. Translated by Arthur Wills. London: Routledge & Kegan Paul, 1956.

———. *Simone Weil*. Edited by Eric O. Springsted. Maryknoll, NY: Orbis, 1998.

———. *Waiting for God*. Translated by Emma Crauford. New York: HarperPerennial, 2009.

———. *Simone Weil: Late Philosophical Writings*. Edited and translated by Eric O. Springsted. Notre Dame, IN: University of Notre Dame Press, 2015.

Williams, Rowan. *Choose Life*. London: Bloomsbury, 2013.

Wiman, Christian. *My Bright Abyss*. New York: Farrar, Strauss and Giroux, 2013.

Williamson, Clark. *A Guest in the House of Israel*. Louisville: Westminster John Knox, 1993.

Name Index

Aeschylus, 97
Antony, Louise, 12–14
Arendt, Hannah, 41
Aristotle, 34, 98, 104, 125
Augustine, 23, 137

Bartholomew, Ecumenical Patriarch, 121
Baudelaire, Charles, 117
Bolz-Weber, Nadia, 60
Bonhoeffer, Dietrich, 94
Borg, Marcus, 25, 31
Bunyan, John, 28

Cahill, Thomas, 84
Camus, Albert, 94
    The Myth of Sisyphus, 7
    The Plague, 46–47, 97, 109
Catherine of Genoa, ix, 5
Cezanne, Paul, 39
Chardin, Teilhard de, 119
Chittister, Joan, 28, 94, 115
Consiglio, Cyprian, 125

David, King of Israel, 42
Descartes, René, 137
Dickinson, Emily, 62, 100
Diekmann, Godfrey, 139
Dillard, Annie, 39, 136
    For the Time Being, 38
    Holy the Firm, 81, 125
    Pilgrim at Tinker Creek, 39–40, 68, 118, 137, 151
    Teaching a Stone to Talk, 115

Drndić, Daša, 108

Eckhart, Meister, 140
Elijah, 41, 56–57
Eliot, George, 101
Elizabeth, mother of John the Baptist, 139
Ellul, Jacques, 131
Euripides, 97

Fox, Matthew, 61

God, *passim*
Greenberg, Irving, 108
Gutting, Gary, 12–13

Hampl, Patricia, 86
Handel, George Friedrich, 16, 114, 122
Haught, John, 120
Hawthorne, Nathaniel, 42
Henry, Patrick, 13
Henry, Patrick G., 149
Heschel, Rabbi Abraham Joshua, 88
Hicks, Edward, 58
Hobbes, Thomas, 129
Holy Spirit, 77, 144, 147
Hopkins, Gerard Manley, 105
Hume, David, 125

Ibsen, Henrik, 63
Illingworth, Garth, 112

James, William, 125

Name Index

Jefferson, Thomas, 105
Jesus, 15, 20, 32–33, 47, 64, 70, 76, 93, 109, 130, 137, 141, 144, 151
    and feeding five thousand, 104–5
    and Good Samaritan parable, 106–8
    and his disciples, 37, 41, 78
    and John the Baptist, 2, 140
    and Mary Magdalene, 42, 132
    and road to Emmaus, 132–34
    and Sadducees, 72
    and Sermon on the Mount, 64, 80–81
    birth of, 44
    transfiguration of, 41–42
Job, 11, 15, 17, 79
John (Jesus' disciple), 37, 41, 132
John the Baptist, 2, 140
Joseph, stepfather of Jesus, 44, 93,

Kahneman, Daniel, 68–69
Kant, Immanuel, 23–24, 115
Kennedy, Robert F., 97
Keshavarz, Fatemeh, 67
Ketcham, Katherine, 85
Kidd, Susan Monk, 35
Kierkegaard, Soren, 112–13
King Jr., Martin Luther, 97
Kipling, Rudyard, 99
Kolbe, Maximillian, 94
Kurtz, Ernest, 85
Kushner, Lawrence, 26

Lamott, Anne, 54, 73, 79
    Bird by Bird, 20
    Plan B, 45, 48
    Small Victories, 62
Lewis, C. S., 82, 85
Lightman, Alan, 110–12
Luther, Martin, 61, 76

MacDonnell, Kilian, 137
Mantel, Hilary, 33–34
Martel, Yann, 91
Mary, Mother of God, 44, 93, 96, 138–40
Mary Magdalene, 42, 132

McKellan, Ian, 51
Mendelssohn, Felix, 56–57
Montaigne, Michel de, 35–37, 100–2
Moses, 23–24, 31, 41, 44–45
Murdoch, Iris, 23, 107
    Existentialists and Mystics, 39, 43, 64, 96
    Metaphysics as a Guide to Morals, 24
    Nuns and Soldiers, 141

Nashishibi, Rami, 65
Newman, John Henry, 62
Newton, John, 99
Nietzsche, Friedrich, 147
Norris, Kathleen, x, 52, 91, 133–34

O'Connor, Flannery, 84

Pascal, Blaise, 111–12
Paul (apostle), 64–65, 126, 145
Penny, Louise, vi
Peter (Jesus' disciple), 37, 41–42, 78, 132
Plato, x, 23, 34, 137
Polkinghorne, John, 117, 121–22
Pope Francis, 117

Renoir, Pierre-Auguste, 117
Rilke, Rainer Maria, 39
Robinson, Marilynne, 25, 87, 122

Shakespeare, William, 50–51, 130, 147
Socrates, 64, 96, 100, 120
Sophocles, 97

Taylor, Barbara Brown, 79
Thomas (Jesus' disciple), 37–38
Tippett, Krista, 65, 119
Tolkien, J.R.R., 5, 146
Trocme, Andre and Magda, 16
Twain, Mark, 14, 73

Udin, Sala, 98
Uzzah, 7, 42

Name Index

Voltaire, 20, 24

Weil, Simone, 48, 94, 115, 149
    Gravity and Grace, 7, 62
    Notebooks, 103
    The Need for Roots, 24
    Waiting for God, 16, 48–49, 107, 120, 121, 150
Wilberforce, William, 99
Williams, Rowan, 30, 117
Wiman, Christian, 33–35, 66–67, 78–79

Zipporah, 44

Scripture Index

OLD TESTAMENT

Exodus
3:3	44
20:4	24
20:18–19	23
32:14	24, 32

Second Samuel
6:1–7	42
6:6–8	7

First Kings
19:4	57

Job
14:1–12	15
19:25–26	17
42:5	11

Psalms
5:1–3	88
8:3–4	104
33:7	116
34:8	26
37:4–5, 7	57
42:1–3	67
42:8	116
46:1–4	116
46:10	51, 86
51:5	61
51:10, 12	66
62:9	53
69:2–3	116
84:3	117
119:11	148
129:3	126
131:2	52, 59
149:4	87

Ecclesiastes
3:8	59

Isaiah
2:4	58
11:6–8	58
58:3, 5–7	109
61:1	92
61:3	4

Jeremiah
15:16	149
17:9	66

Lamentations
3:21–26	126

Micah
6:8	106

Scripture Index

Zephaniah

3:20	131

NEW TESTAMENT

Matthew

5:1–11	80
5:48	64
14:31	78

Mark

9:3	41

Luke

1:28	138
1:34	138
1:48	139
4:18	93
4:21	93
9:28–36	41
9:60	72
10:30–37	95
10:31	106
10:35	106
10:37	106
17:21	59
20:27–38	72
24:21	132

John

3:8	78
4:14	70
6:35	70
8:32	32
9:25	130
14:6	33
20:17	42
20:19	37
20:24	37
20:28	38
20:29	37

Romans

7:15, 18–19, 24	64
7:18	61
8:1–3	65
8:18	9

First Corinthians

13:13	126
15:20	17

Ephesians

6:17	145

Hebrews

10:31	24
11:1	74, 130

Second Peter

3:9	8

www.ingramcontent.com/pod-product-compliance
Lightning Source LLC
Chambersburg PA
CBHW031434150426
43191CB00006B/510